COPPER, IRON, AND CLAY

COPPER, IRON, AND CLAY

A SMITH'S JOURNEY

SARA DAHMEN

wm

WILLIAM MORROW

An Imprint of HarperCollins*Publishers*

⊱⊱⊰⊰⊰

Uncle Doug and me, with a tree we planted on his land in North Carolina.
The hill is now covered in riotous bamboo, which he also planted.

⊱⊱⊰⊰⊰

CONTENTS

Cooking in copper out in Portland, Oregon. Fire and food happen everywhere!

PREFACE

I have a question for you: *What are you cooking on?*

What is it actually made of? Where was it made? Who made it? How long will it last? Like most of us, you probably have no idea where your cookware is from (other than the big-box store or catalog where you purchased it). I didn't either, for a really long time.

We care so much about the food we're eating and where it came from. Let's take it a step further. Why are we cooking that fantastic, organic food in a pan coated with unknown elements? Why don't we look at cookware the way we look at our food choices? Why do we purchase cookware made with mystery chemicals but insist our vegetables are grown pesticide-free? Why do we accept that our pots fall apart and clutter landfills but protest the tons of plastic food wrappings tossed every day?

We need to take cookware to the next level. It's time to understand your cookware. Ask questions. Demand transparency, efficiency, and provenance.

I personally believe a discussion about cookware is part of the conversation about food. If we're demanding to know if our food is made locally and with the least impact on the environment, we should expect the same of our cookware. We should care about where the molecular change happens to our food and be able to get answers about the "ingredients" in our pots and pans. The easiest way to do that is sometimes to go back to the beginning: Know who made your cookware, what it is made from, and why you are using it today.

You deserve that knowledge.

Cook well, and cook with meaning.

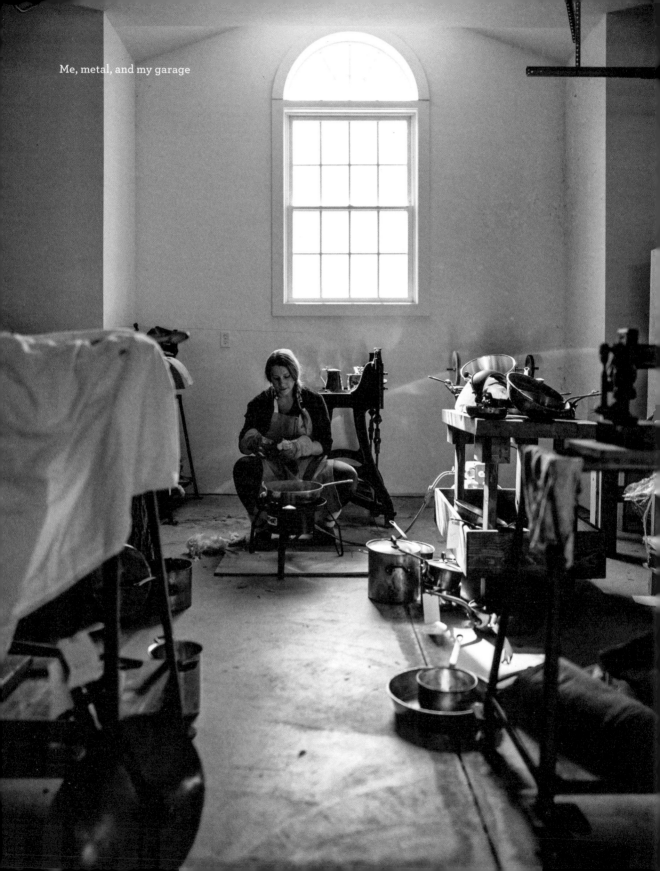

INTRODUCTION

The first burn I remember getting was in my uncle's forge in the hidden hills of North Carolina backcountry, where greenery drips on top of greenery in the summer. The smash and ping of Uncle Doug's hammer echoed and bounced between the steep slopes of the mountains on the edge of the Cherokee National Forest.

Like those true craftsmen of old, Uncle Doug had a spacious forge connected to the cement and aluminum box of a house where he lived with my aunt. The forge's giant doors swung open to the elements to let the fire's heat escape. Everything was covered with fluffy black soot and smelled of coal, leather, and dust.

I was just about to start twelfth grade and was visiting with my parents and brothers when I gamely said I wanted to try my hand at making a piece of wrought iron. I have no recollection of what I made. A nail? A cross? I still have the scar from the burn on my left index finger. It was a harbinger of things to come decades later, when I fell in love with fire and heat. But at seventeen I did it more to humor Uncle Doug and give my mother a good subject for action shots of our visit. Uncle Doug had fresh aloe planted near the door, facing the sunlight, and I spent the rest of the day's visit with a gooey stick plastered to my finger, far away from the fire. I'm glad I tried it, as the memory brings a big smile; sadly, my uncle died suddenly on March 30, 2019.

Other than brief trips to Uncle Doug's house and forge, metal wasn't part of my life at all. After college, I dove into advertising and marketing like a properly raised woman determined to use her education. My marriage at age twenty-two to John, my college sweetheart, brought me closer to metal, if only by way of my in-laws: My father-in-law made a living at the time by welding. In his basement he would build everything from the toy chests in my children's rooms to impossibly tall birdhouses and fantastical creatures made from leftover scrap metal.

A trip to Uncle Doug's forge in 2001, when I received that very first metal burn

I spent my days hard at work at an ad agency and my evenings moonlighting as a wedding planner while John studied for finance tests. The closest I came to cookware was when I cooked in our tiny one-bedroom apartment in Milwaukee. The kitchen had a gas stove that needed to be lit with a match, and the eating area was so small we could only fit one of those outdoor bistro tables and two chairs in it. Our wedding china remained in boxes in our parents' basements. I had a handful of pots and pans, which barely fit in cupboards jammed with our wedding gifts, plus some cheap nonstick pots from when I'd been holed up in a minuscule efficiency apartment before John and I tied the knot. This was the best we could manage, and it didn't deter me from having dinner parties, though looking back, I wonder what I thought I was accomplishing by cramming even two more bodies into that tiny kitchen and eating area.

Shortly after John and I bought a house outside Milwaukee, the real estate market crashed in 2008. No one knew the extent of the damage at first or how much it would affect nearly every industry. Also, anything that happens on the coasts seems to show up later in the Midwest, so while we didn't feel the immediate dramatic effects of the crash the way they may have in New York, our recovery was going to take far, far longer. Because of this "slow crash," I didn't think it strange to make a huge life change right then, so I left my steady job with benefits at the ad agency to strike out on my own as a full-time event planner. John would say it was because I never do anything the easy way!

Being a wedding planner did have its perks. Not only did I get to work with people who were usually extremely passionate about their marriage beyond the wedding day itself, but I was also able to design beautiful moments for them. Plus, I loved the tastings and food choices!

I could probably write a book about the event catastrophes that happened. ("Um . . . the cake topper fell in the catering room and the bride's head broke off," and "The entire tent has collapsed in the thunderstorm," and even "I know it's four days before the wedding and you're almost due with a baby, but the maharajah horse the groom needed for the ceremony just died!") Still, I really loved doing weddings and events and met many wonderful people who are still friends today.

Wedding planning requires more physical engagement than what is shown on television—there are silk banners to be stretched across log cabin arches, flower crowns to be glued, candles to be hung from silvery branches, and glittery name tags to be set out by every place setting. And sometimes there are last-minute panics:

"The bride wants to toss the bouquet!"

"She doesn't have a toss bouquet. She didn't want one."

"Well, you better do something or she's going to throw that ten-pound arrangement and hurt somebody!"

Cue my hastily pulling flowers from a centerpiece, tying them with grass, and praying they stayed together. Moments like that leave a body feeling fresh and alive.

Plus, I always love a challenge—the thrill of creative problem solving.

Then the children came. First I simply carried Will along to every meeting. Looking back, I can't believe I'd take him to restaurants where I'd sit with an engaged couple while nursing and taking notes and then run to a rehearsal with him in tow, leaving him hanging out in a church aisle while I sprinted around to take care of some problem. No wonder he's a chill kid!

When Hannah came along two years later, I took her to most meetings, too. Though I did try to coordinate fewer weddings, I wasn't exactly slowing down; between working as a mom and a wedding planner, I had two full-time jobs simultaneously. In the meantime, John was eyeballs-deep in studying for his chartered financial analyst certification, so things were always a little crazy around the house.

John and I had always planned to have lots of kids. When we were dating, we initially thought six, but that soon became five. Once we realized how expensive raising children can be, and the amount of mental and physical energy that is required to take care of tiny human beings, the number was chiseled to four. After we had Hannah, we wavered. Four or three?

Getting pregnant and having another child proved to be far more difficult than we anticipated. It slowly became likely that I'd keep miscarrying instead of filling our bedrooms with little ones. We hoped for a third baby while friends and family (thirty-two women, to be exact) became pregnant and had babies. To stave off a growing panic and looming depression, I first spoke to a therapist but then decided writing fiction would focus my energy on something that didn't have to do with babies (or lack of a positive pregnancy test). I've always loved old stories, so without much of a plan, I sat down at my computer and my first work of historical fiction shot out of me in a matter of weeks.

The healing had begun: I buried myself in researching the people of the old West, the foods they ate, and the clothes they wore, and I focused less on my personal trauma. As the adage goes, once you stop watching the teakettle, it whistles. About nine months after I finished the novel, Jack was born.

What I'd absorbed in those cozy evenings of research embedded itself into my bones. I learned about food and cooking in the 1800s and fell in love with the ways of that time. I now knew what kinds of items could be found in a traditional pioneer kitchen. There were glossy, well-worn cast-iron griddles and ovens, handmade copper pots and canteens, and fat, painted stoneware bowls. I knew the spoons would have been stained, the wood well-seasoned, the fancy tea services likely to be tin covered in black asphaltum and hand-painted with flowers in thick, wide strokes. I understood how a single pot would have been carefully groomed for the next generation and that a woman would have been able to cook a roast or stew and bake bread or pie all in the same cast-iron skillet. These pioneer tools became tactile to me as I wrote my stories. The frontier kitchens were in my blood. They felt solid, as if the history of the past were tangible today.

It made me wonder . . . if a vintage pot could talk, what would it say? Would it tell me about meals cooked over a fire in the prairie? Would it divulge the secrets of a winter's night, with twelve children huddled around the hearth for both warmth and food?

My experience at Uncle Doug's house wasn't unusual; my parents wanted my two younger brothers and me to have a large helping of hands-on experiences as children. We would often go to fur trade and frontier reenactments held in the small towns and villages of heavily forested northern Wisconsin where I grew up. I remember the distinct atmosphere of joy and contentment as I watched the ladies cook around their campfires. And even though the cooper might have been grumpy as he made wooden buckets, and I burned my fingers making candles, I remember fondly the long dresses the women wore, the relaxation of creamy canvas tents swaying between the pines in the forest where the reenactors set up camp. And I watched with envy as the women called in the men from their trades, or the children from running barefoot along the dirt paths, and sat down in the late, buttery sunlight for dinner as if 1829 were still happening in front of my eyes.

All those moments came into my head as I wrote fiction, and maybe that was part of the catalyst that made me start a new career, even though I didn't realize what was happening at the time. Between writing fiction and reminiscing about those soft, warm family memories, I decided rather suddenly that I wanted to create a line of cookware like what Paul Revere would have made. I knew I wanted several different types of cookware, which would include various items made of pottery, cast iron, and copper. While sourcing all these items became challenging from the very beginning, the copper cookware was by far the most intriguing part of the cookware line, and it excited me the most.

A reproduction of a traditional cast-iron skillet, smoke ring and all

But the original copperware made by copper- and tinsmiths in America had mostly disappeared and the industry was all but defunct. A lot of cast iron was mass-produced overseas, as were ceramics. Many large-scale manufacturers had gone out of business, so most people keeping these homegrown crafts alive were boutique artisans hidden away in small crafting communities or on hobby farms. The copper kettles carried overland by burly fur traders and voyagers and given or traded with Indigenous people? Those kettles were not part of any kitchen I knew anymore. Very few people even knew what they looked like. The "spider skillets" of early America or those created with the smoke ring along the bottom to fit the American potbellied stove? Maybe on eBay. These designs—which were, at their deepest heart, American—were *gone*.

Before the twentieth century, cookware was pure and simple. It was made completely of clay, iron, and soft metals such as copper and tin. There were no plastics sprayed on the pans, no paint, and no strange concoctions of different enzymes and complicated alloys. Cookware was made organically and with natural elements from the land. Likely it was made by one of your neighbors. It was basic.

But in the early 1900s, cooking schools had started using aluminum and stainless steel in their classes, especially after the Ideal Home Exhibition in the United Kingdom in 1909 unveiled a plethora of steel cookware. By the time Teflon came around in the mid-1940s, stainless steel had taken the place of copper and cast iron in the kitchen. Stainless was considered a prestigious commodity because of its use during World War I and World War II. Today many people still assume they should pay quite a decent amount of money for a good, thick set of stainless steel, even though it is not expensive to make this cookware. That mentality is born from a generational understanding of the "specialness" of stainless, which was due to the war effort and need. Crazy how our battles from decades ago still influence our choices in metals!

But although aluminum and stainless-steel cookware took over most tasks in the kitchen, heirloom pieces of cast iron and even copper were still handed down across generations, going from kitchen to kitchen and stowed away in dusty basements. (I would like to point out that cast-iron

A vintage wrought-iron pot, made in sections. The marks of the wax and sprue for pouring in the iron are still visible.

cooking never fully went out of style, even if it was sometimes cloaked in enamel or porcelain.) And as for clay and ceramics, think of how they have been part of our hearths and flames for ten thousand years and yet somehow have become a dowdy auntie compared with copper and iron. But we still fall back on a solid piece of earth for the perfect pie pan—that's strong history right there.

I started to wonder if I was the only one feeling nostalgic about these lost historic items. Our great-grandmothers used them and maybe our grandmothers, too. Didn't that type of dedication to historical kitchenware mean anything? Did anyone else want beautiful copper pieces back in their kitchens? Wouldn't people prefer to buy a hand-fired cast-iron skillet over a mass-produced one? Did people wonder whether the clay in their pie plate was local? I decided that if I loved historical cookware, maybe other people would, too.

But then I had to ask myself: *What did I want to make? How would I do it, and how would I source the materials? Who could help me?* My hope was to talk to local artisans in the United States, although I didn't have a single clue where to start or what questions to ask. It turns out that finding artisans in family-owned and -operated businesses who were willing to teach the ins and outs of their trade was tougher than I thought.

It didn't help that I was determined to design along the lines of traditional cookware, many of which were no longer in circulation or commonly found in stores. The shapes that had long been used by our ancestors had been lost or forgotten or were considered archaic. The actual materials were also nearly extinct. One can find beautiful pieces of cookware from overseas, but they may not be made with the original metals once prized in cookware. Deciding on the shapes I wanted to re-create took a lot more research than I expected, too, from scouring the internet to paging through out-of-print books found on dusty bottom shelves in used bookstores. These were shapes once made by American coppersmiths and their apprentices, usually modified from original European patterns, and all of them—especially the copper—could be found only occasionally as vintage pieces.

At the same time I was searching to find local artisans, the bigger national conversation about food and purity circulated nonstop. As I planned

An oval copper piece. This cookware was made "in the flat" from sheets of copper by hand and finished with blacksmith-made wrought-iron handles. This type of craftsmanship typically dates a piece like this to the 1700s or early 1800s.

my cookware line, I hoped the passion behind the notion itself—to create real, local, pure metal cookware—would be well received in the circles of people who care so deeply about their food. I hoped to add to the conversation.

I wanted to start by building copper cookware, and I could find only one other company in America trying to do a similar thing. I sent them an email, hoping to get any advice at all, as I still didn't really know what to ask for. I didn't think "Hi, stranger, tell me your trade secrets!" would go very far. But I was beyond fortunate. Mac Kohler, owner of Brooklyn Copper Cookware, agreed to answer my questions and led me down a road of mentorship I couldn't have found had I tried any other way.

In those first stirringly beautiful conversations, Mac reinforced my belief that there was a market for pure copper cookware made in America, not least because no one else was doing it. We agreed that while we would be competing, our pots and pans were so aesthetically different that we weren't in direct competition, and Mac made sure I had a proper list of qualities I should look for in a customer: a foodie, a reader of cookbooks and food blogs, someone who is engaged in learning about their food and their cookware. And we both inherently wanted to make something built to last, never to be found in a landfill. We wanted to make treasures. Mac wasn't selling his wares at this time either. He, too, was building his company and the designs of his pot handles and bodies—he was just much further along in his process than I was.

Historical research gave me ideas on what I wanted the cookware to look like—the copper cookware of the original fur traders and early American coppersmiths—but that was about it. I had napkin sketches and a few pictures from the internet. But I need to reiterate: I knew *nothing*.

Working from the information I'd absorbed from Mac, I started searching for vendors to help me make everything from handles to rivets. This involved saying over and over, "Hi! I want to make this, but I have no idea what I'm doing!" There were many pieces of the cookware to find. For instance, I needed someone to pour handles to specifications I'd determined were traditional Americana and do it with a certain grade of iron for the copper cookware. I wanted to produce solid, real pots and pans and accompanying goods that were steeped in history, formed in long-lost shapes, and made in the most local way possible. And I slowly started to ask more questions. Why couldn't we get our cookware made locally anymore? Why was it hard to find? Why did commercial, store-bought pots and pans promise the moon and then fail?

Since no one was really asking these questions, it was hard to find an articulate answer. Still, after a lot of calls, I started to learn what to ask for:

Do you do small-batch manufacturing? Like, say I want only one hundred pieces . . .

Are there setup fees? If I want only fifty instead of five thousand, will it be too pricey?

What kind of tooling is needed? Do you make the tools for the pieces in-house?

It was baptism by fire. Mac took me under his wing and washed tons of knowledge over me, and eventually some of it stuck. The rest I had to fake or say "Sure!" and research later. I called Uncle Doug in North Carolina to ask him about metals. A woman who was only an acquaintance at the time said, "You know, I can take your sketches and put them into CAD [computer-aided design software]—that's my job!" Suddenly I had a product developer—and Julia became a dear friend. My kids had to listen to me talk about thermal conductivity while I taught myself exactly what that was. With his finance background, John dug into the COGS (cost of goods sold): How much of our savings would be eaten?

My search to locate actual heirloom cookware makers fizzled quickly. Why? The answer was simple and devastating: *What was once available for purchase from local artisans down the street simply no longer existed.* Family businesses had all but disappeared. The trades and crafts of copper cookware making and hand-tinning were nearly gone. Cast-iron foundries made engine parts but not kitchen items; they were uncertain if pots could be poured exactly to my specs. And forget about finding a brass foundry for handles. It felt like I was searching for a needle in a haystack—when someone had already removed the needle.

It wasn't even so much that the artisans and craftspeople were few and far between; the absolute void of knowledge was astounding. How had we lost so much of our culture in just a few short decades? Did we as consumers care so little about our cookware? While there is a distinct foodie culture now that covets vintage pots and will spend money on special pans, it's a relatively new phenomenon, which to my delight is growing stronger every day. As a culture, we once created and treasured these items together in our communities, because it was a way of life, not just a trend. Today we can buy expensive cooking tools to make specialized dishes, such as immersion circulators for cooking sous vide, but they're probably made in another country. It's hard to find real, solid, fine cookware made locally anymore. If you want the good stuff, you really have to go hunting.

My first break in finding artisans turned out to be right up the road from me in Kaukauna, Wisconsin. Roloff Foundry is a small 100 percent family-

Sparks from the cast-iron "charge," the molten mix of metals in the furnace in Roloff Foundry

owned and -operated cast-iron foundry that makes small batches of pans for another cast-iron designer in Wisconsin. When I reached out to them, they said, "Sure! Come on up!"

"Can I bring my kids?"

"Um. No."

"Damn, I need to find a sitter!"

A few weeks later, I headed on up, dressing for what I thought would be a formal meeting. I'd been to Uncle Doug's forge, of course, but hey, I figured I needed to project business smarts by wearing a blazer and some cute shoes.

When I arrived at the foundry, the men were wearing flannel, hardhats, and steel-toe boots. Brad and Jeff, who manage new business, engineering, and everything in between, and Dave, the owner, met me in the office, gray around the edges from the dust of the foundry floor. They all looked at me, then at my shoes, and it was very clear by the expressions flitting across their faces that I had flunked an important test.

"We, ah, were going to give you a tour, but your shoes . . ."

I figured I'd act tough, like my shoe choice wasn't a big deal. "Oh, it's okay. They can get dirty."

"Yeah . . . but . . ." It seemed they were torn between safety, trying not to point out my naiveté, and pleasing a client. "Maybe we won't go by the molten iron?"

The foundry was nothing like Uncle Doug's forge. If you've never walked through one, know this: They are hot, they are loud, and three inches of black and charcoal soot cover every single surface. It's unavoidable, and it's everywhere. I was suddenly walking in my pretty little ballet flats through iron flakes and pretending I wasn't freaked out at all.

To their credit, they now tease me about that day. And they were gracious enough to always treat me like I knew what I was doing.

Mac and I go back to the beginning, when I was first trying to learn about copper and speak to those who would have the knowledge to help make my idea a reality. He could have ignored me. He didn't have to spend time teaching me about copperware or offering big vocabulary words about metalsmithing or how tin and copper bond. But he did, and he helped open my eyes to the amazing feats copper can do in the kitchen.

What is likely the biggest influence in a person's draw to copper cookware? The romanticism? The science? The efficacy? All of the above?

The draw to pure copper is assembled out of clues that people who love to cook find as they nurture their passion, usually over years and while using many other kinds of cookware. Perhaps they watched Julia Child on television and noticed that she not only used copper cookware in her demonstrations but also had an entire wall of it behind her. Often while dining at better restaurants, well-used copper will be in evidence in the kitchen. Copper is found in the still-life paintings of the Old Masters.

Modern manufacturers of stainless-steel cookware are also observed tacitly endorsing copper's advantages by sandwiching bits of it into their designs with the hope of convincing prospective customers that their wares harness copper's performance at a lower price. This mimicry is taken to an absurd degree in the form of cheap stamped aluminum pans with flimsy copper-colored polymer coatings being passed off as "copper infused." Nonetheless, the message is that copper is as good as it gets.

After a short time using that first pan, copper usually becomes the default choice for additions to the *batterie* [*batterie de cuisine* is a French term for describing a full set of cookware], slowly replacing lower-performance wares. Care and maintenance of tin-lined copper becomes part of an increasingly enjoyable ritual of cooking, much like sharpening one's knives or seasoning the cast iron.

The attraction to copper happens in the manner of a seduction. Like sophisticated foods, the most seductive things are simply composed of few and pure materials, easily understood, mature in taste, and meant to be enjoyed conscientiously.

How do you believe copperware adds to the cookware discussion as a whole?

Much as it's added to other metals to mimic the performance of the pure stuff, copper stands as a reference and a touchstone. Copper is the standard to beat for other modern cookware materials. In a less measurable dimension, copper cookware stands for a principle of renewability and multigenerational durability that transcends its status as a simple household tool.

Copper cookware makes a contribution to any contemporaneous discussion about cooking in a way that is difficult, if not impossible, for other cookware materials: conscientiously and in a sustainable way. Before it becomes a pan, copper's carbon footprint is small, taking far less energy to smelt than aluminum or stainless steel. And unlike polymerized petrochemicals, pure tin is utterly nontoxic, high performance, and, in the event of damage or wear, completely renewable.

From its entry into service, a piece of copper cookware carries with it the potential to be a gift to future generations, not merely manifestly as a restorable cooking tool but also as an heirloom that helped sustain the generation making the gift and as a human artifact that did not end up in a landfill.

As a manufacturer, what are the hurdles that come with creating copper cookware from scratch?

Copper cookware was made in the United States before it was the United States. Recall that Paul Revere was a coppersmith. As skilled trades, soft-metal spinning and hand-tinning were relatively common in the century between the American Civil War and World War II, and copper cookware enjoyed a surge of popularity in the early second half of the twentieth century.

The skills needed to make quality copper cookware were quietly displaced by the advent of automated mass-production methods and the repurposing of war material production to peace-time markets, a process that extended from the 1950s to the 1970s. By the end of the 1970s, cheaply stamped, nonstick aluminum had taken over the cookware market and was being sold by advertising rather than by knowledgeable staff in cookware shops.

With the collapse of the high end of the market went the skills to make cookware by hand using the best materials. Certain of the necessary skills for making copper cookware were applied to other manufacturing tasks, often subassemblies for larger goods, but by the early twenty-first century no company in the United States hosted the entire skill set for making one of the oldest technologies known to humanity, tin-lined copper cookware.

The major difficulty was keeping faith: Because the United States had produced world-class copper cookware in the past, we continued to believe we could do it today. Building the cookware one hundred percent from scratch meant building a supply chain entirely from the ground up. We needed a kitchen before we could cook anything up.

What do you personally find so alluring about copper?

What first persuaded me about tin-lined copper (I collected for nearly twenty years before starting BCC [Brooklyn Copper Cookware]) was how responsive it was and how in very little time I stopped second-guessing and compensating for my tools. Copper is very easy to use well and, when trying new or unfamiliar techniques, is a rock-steady constant—it does what it purports to do, and I do not have to think about it. This realization freed me to play more with cooking, to experiment, to improve, and mostly to relax.

Once my pots and pans were working with me in simple, uncomplicated support of my cooking, my patience with my other tools (many of them inherited or sentimental favorites) wore quickly thin, and I educated myself on where I could make improvements. Using copper cookware began an across-the-board kitchen upgrade that took many years of careful sourcing to reveal what it was I could now feel I was after: not the most expensive, certainly not the most popular, but the most passionately and thoughtfully made tools, tools in which I could clearly discern the touch of the maker.

In our age, commodification and industrial processes have gone far to reduce the unit labor costs of bringing anything to market, and for something like a printed circuit board, that's probably okay. However, there are some things we do to sustain ourselves, impart meaning to life, and remind us of our humanity that benefit by maximizing unit labor costs (i.e., by having as many hands in the mix as possible). I think our daily bread is among those things. To me, copper is capable of conducting those energies easily as well as it does heat.

It took almost a year, but eventually I had cast-iron pots in full development and a local potter lined up to produce stoneware pieces for me, even though I had started with the copper development first. It helped that cast-iron foundries are more plentiful in Wisconsin, and there are pockets of pottery artisans around as well. I was excited to be using local Wisconsin and midwestern artisans, and I hoped they were all glad to work with me and my harebrained idea of creating a cookware line from scratch. My kids were slowly getting easier to handle, and luckily they still all napped at the same time every day. So I had time to continue my cold calls to find makers of copper cookware components, a prerequisite for fulfilling my ultimate goal of creating a line of copper cookware.

I spoke to countless makers, foundries, tool-and-die creators, designers, rivet manufacturers, and machinists. Every time I'd pick up the phone to call yet another potential business collaborator, I'd take a deep breath and hope they didn't ask me a question I couldn't answer. But over time those cold calls were the biggest piece of my education in learning to speak about metals. I paid attention to the conversations and kept a piece of paper nearby so that I could jot down terms and processes for later research, and I was unafraid to ask questions, no matter how fundamental. Anyone can go online and start to put together basic information about a field, but the real knowledge comes from those who live and work in their trade every day. Gleaning tidbits from every conversation, combining those Post-its, checking library books, and rereading my notes slowly gave me power when I wanted to speak to artisans and makers. Eventually I stopped sounding quite so ignorant.

My Polish German tenacity (some would call it stubbornness) kept me going. Every week I made phone calls or sent out emails. In the beginning, those phone calls typically went like this: "Hi! I don't know if you can help me, but I want to make copper pots!" There was typically a long, slow intake of air, and I could almost hear whoever picked up the phone shake their head on the other end of the line. "Oooh, yeah, we don't do that. We don't work on copper at all."

"Do you know anyone who does?" I'd ask, fingers crossed.

"Ahhhh, no. No, I don't. I don't even know where to send you."

I've lost track of how often I heard that type of response, but it's still burned into my head.

In the meantime, Mac had found a family-owned and -operated company in Dayton, Ohio, that was willing to learn how to spin his copper cookware, and he later generously passed their name on to me. We spoke often and discussed our projects to make sure we didn't create similar items. This allowed us to compete in a general sense but still have a corner of the American-made copper cookware market all to ourselves. And in the end, the collaborative spirit helped us both create the wares we wanted.

Before I went to visit the fabricators who would spin the copper, I bought a pair of steel-toe boots. They were clean and perfect when I arrived at Ohio Metal Fabricating. Plus, I received compliments on them from the gals in the office. Score one point!

To collaborate with Ohio Metal in creating the tooling for the copper body components, I had to head down to Dayton, shake hands, get a factory tour, and chat with the guys about the pots. They were new to the process, too, having worked with Mac only a short time to try to figure out if they could spin copper cookware. Gary (the owner of Ohio Metal, whom they call Gary Without because he's bald) and Gary (the salesperson, whom they call Gary With because, well, he has a thick head of hair) were up for the challenge, though. When I arrived, we all spent time looking at all the options for making the pots. I told the Garys how excited I was to be working with Ohio Metal, and they shrugged.

"We always say we'll try anything," one of the Garys said.

"Well, thank God!" I responded.

From the moment I got to the fabrication plant and saw the shiny, glowing copper, I knew this was what I wanted to make more than anything else. Copper was to be the crown jewel of my cookware line. It looked outrageously gorgeous and bright. I loved that copper was steeped in history and that it wouldn't rust. Even though I still didn't own any copper cookware myself other than the prototypes of my own line, I vowed to have it ready and available when my cookware line would be fully on the internet.

Sometimes people ask me why I wanted to do everything here in America and why I created "new" designs (that is, bring back those that had

Some vintage-ish copper on display.
Stockpots are always so versatile!

been lost and forgotten) when today's pot and pan designs have worked just fine these past years. Why not just become an importer of pots already created in Europe or mass-produce them in another country to make the price points palatable to big-box stores?

Well, beyond the desire to bring back forgotten aesthetics and to feel connected to the American coppersmiths across the country who are lost to time and history, I really wanted to re-create the traditional pioneer kitchen with the exact metals used back in the 1800s, because it was healthier, traditionally basic, and made sense to me as a person who already cared about the food my family and I ate. We weren't asking what the cookware was made from and who was making it. We didn't understand the shapes we were using and that trends were making decisions for us, not history. Through research for my historical novels, I started to realize that today's "natural" cookware or ceramic-coated pieces were simply fads that helped increase the amount of trash in landfills as these pieces eventually failed. The old designs weren't broken; they'd been used for centuries because they worked and served the purpose they were designed for—to cook well and efficiently. Maybe we'd gotten a bit impatient. It was time to take a breath and slow down.

My passion for cookware and the tidbits of information arrived slowly and organically, pieced together from observing how I monitored our children's foods, researching what had been used in the past for cooking and for food, and a side obsession with history. I wanted to go back to the beginning and use what had sufficed before commercialism may have gotten the better of us.

I want us all to ask, "What am I cooking on?"

I want to talk about the provenance of cookware and the metals that make it, just as we do about the diets of beef cows and the substances put into chicken feed. We try to eat healthy, to shop around for the right food, and, if we are lucky, to make it local and organic. I live in Wisconsin and am surrounded by dozens of farms both small and large and still have to pay attention because there's no guarantee the local food is grown sustainably. Our farms can be massive, supplying thousands of gallons of milk to big cheesemakers, and they aren't always organic just because they're up the road. The farm business to the north of our house springs up out of the flat fields of crops surrounding it, like a silver Emerald City. When we stop in, the cheese curds are sure to be fresh and squeaky, and sometimes covered with dill, but I don't know what their cows are fed.

Other farms are just about produce. Some spray weed killer and fertilizer, some don't. We don't have the miles of strawberries you'll find in California, but we do have mom-and-pop businesses where we can go pick our own berries when they're in their short growing season and some of the farms are fully organic. We once had friends visit from the East Coast, and we took them to the little Appleland farm up the road, where the strawberries were ripe for picking. Our friends asked what kind of shoes they should wear, and I realized they'd never been to a strawberry field. I had always assumed everyone had done such a thing at least once in their life—it's the way of life here in Wisconsin. Our friends were amazed, and no wonder. There's nothing better than picking a ruby red jewel of a berry, sweet and sun ripened, and popping it directly into your mouth.

Farmers' markets have become commonplace even in cities, but you still have to search for produce that's fresh, in-season, and organic. Why do we do this? Why do we put so much work into foraging and hunting for the "right" food, even if it's down the aisles of a supermarket?

We do it for ourselves and also for our families and loved ones. We do it because we want to offer the best, to fill our stomachs with nutritious food, and we want to be able to afford to do it all the time. It's a fair request to make.

We need to think the same way about our cookware to complete the circle. Will our pots and pans end up in a landfill, because they're made with a hodgepodge of materials designed to be inexpensive but that fall apart after less than a decade or two? Why not look at cookware the way we do organic, sustainable food sources? When we buy, shouldn't we be able to ask, Is it made with pure materials, and is this heirloom quality? Our selection of kitchen tools should be as conscious a decision as it is with our food.

An apocryphal story my mother once told me explains a bit how information about our cookware and cooking can get lost over just a few decades. A young woman prepared a roast for her new husband. He asked her why she cut the ends off of the roast before putting it in the oven.

"It's perfectly good meat," he argued.

She replied, "It's just how my mother always did it, and I learned it from her."

She later called her mother and asked why the ends of the roast were always cut off, and her mother said, "Why, I learned it from *my* mother. I have no idea why the recipe is made that way."

After hanging up with her daughter, her mother rang the elderly family matriarch and asked the same question.

"Oh, well, I had a tiny ceramic baking dish back then. I always had to cut off the ends to make the meat fit in it," the old woman said. "I just got used to doing it that way, even when I eventually could afford bigger cookware."

Dare to question what we are cooking on, and why.

I wanted to have some semblance of control over the entire creative cookware-building process and to work with small, family artisans. It was important to me to be able to shake the hands of everyone working on the cookware. I wanted the process to feel as alive and true now as it did back in the day, when you'd walk down the street to buy crockery from a local shop where it was handmade. This whole philosophy would eventually mean getting my hands literally into the thick of it, though I certainly never was going to attempt to make all the cookware myself. I'm no potter, so the clay and stoneware would always have to be made by other, more expert hands.

With such a mind-set, though, I had chosen a much harder road. Every time I turned around, another challenge, another change, another decision popped up, and I was completely and utterly winging it. Daily, I'd ask myself, "What am I *doing*?" while trying to keep things floating and balanced with my normal life.

What made copper pot construction less stressful than it might have been was that everyone in Ohio dealt so kindly with me and pretended I knew what I was doing. Just as in the first foundry I worked with in Wisconsin, the guys creating the copperware and the gals running the office treated me like an equal, which bolstered my confidence and kept me feeling less like an imbecile when I did pick up the phone or come to a meeting and start asking questions.

Still, conversations went something like this for the first two years:

FABRICATOR: So I guess we could build the tool out of 4140.

ME [*I have no clue what that is*]: Ah. Good. You think that will work?

FABRICATOR: Sure. And it's pretty soft, so if you need to harden it later, we still can.

ME [*nodding with a serious face*]: Hmm. Okay. I guess if we can harden it later, that gives us options. Um. How many can we spin on the, ah . . . the 4140?

THEY SHRUG: Oh, five hundred thousand pots.

ME [*I will never make that many copper pots ever, and no matter what this 4140 is, it sounds like they know what they are doing, even if I don't quite yet!*]: I think we'll be fine. Let's go with that.

Like most things with my cookware journey, everything just happened, like a drop of rain hitting that flat but iridescent surface of a pond, shuddering, and then spreading outward.

Figuring out the designs took more work than simply drawing pictures on a napkin and showing my friend Julia, who could put things into the computer and measure them exactly. There were technical questions to be resolved, such as the ratio of size and thickness of a pot to the material used. I had pulled photographs from old books and held original vintage pieces, but they were just the inspiration. I had to figure out the shapes of handles and the weight balances so the handles wouldn't be too long or heavy for the body of the pot or pan. I had to look at what pottery designs were out there already, figure out exactly what I wanted to bring back to kitchens, and find potters to accommodate those designs. Every step involved more decisions that I didn't always feel qualified to make. For instance, after I had figured out with Ohio Metal the designs of the copper pots themselves, the pots still required handles, which needed to be con-figured, fixed, heat treated, and poured. I also needed someone to regate (restructure the openings where the metal is poured in) the tooling for the copper cookware handles in order to pour ductile iron, since the handles were made of iron that needed to be poured into the molds just like the cast-iron skillets. (*Tooling* and *tools*, by the way, are loose terms used inter-changeably in manufacturing, which confused the hell out of me for about a year. With copper pot making, the *tool* is essentially a steel fixture made to fit onto a CNC [computer numerical control] machine for spinning cop-per sheet. In the case of pouring most types of iron, *tooling* usually refers to a cope and drag plate or a large aluminum sheet with hollowed-out spaces where the iron is poured in.) Mike, the toolmaker in Wisconsin, had orig-inally created the copper cookware handle tooling for regular gray cast iron, like what is used for cast-iron skillets. No dice—they didn't work. I needed a different kind of iron that wouldn't crack during the riveting or tinning process. By this time I had a grasp of the way a foundry worked, so I could make two dozen calls in quick succession and rattle everything off in one breath.

"Hi! Do you have a B&P processing machine that pours ductile, pours from the top, can take an aluminum match plate of sixteen by twenty inches, and heat-treat the pieces to eighteen percent elongation?"

One of the few foundries to get back to me was based in Lodi, California. At first I thought Kevin was only the salesperson—until I visited the foundry months later. I was surprised and thrilled to realize that Kevin was also the owner, and his mother had owned and operated Lodi Ironworks before him. Kevin's daughter and son-in-law work at the business, too, and I had yet an-other awesome tour. This time I remembered my steel-toe boots.

The one small missing piece left was finding a supplier for the copper rivets to attach the handles to the copper bodies. Mac had exhausted the Eastern Seaboard looking for a copper rivet manufacturer. He called me from New York and let out a slow, frustrated breath.

"I can't find anyone at all who can make the solid-shank, cold-forged, truss-head CDA 110 electrolytic rivets we need! No one even keeps the wire in stock!"

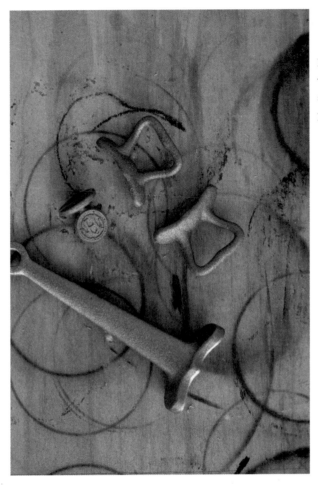

Ductile iron handles were the ticket to some cookware production success!

Enter that Polish German stubbornness again. "Let me look around," I said.

Since we were helping each other fulfill our shared dream of making copper cookware in America, it felt good to be able to contribute something useful to his business in thanks for the mentorship he'd been showing me. No way did I (or Mac) want to have to head to Brazil or China for this last tiny piece. It went against the whole philosophy we shared.

My first call was to Uncle Doug, who gave me some leads. Those leads became more phone calls, and eventually I tripped over someone in my own backyard.

Prairie Rivet is buried in tiny Markesan, Wisconsin. I had to find it on a

Hard-to-find real copper rivets were the final key piece.

map. But its limited website said the company provided copper rivets, so on a wish and a prayer I picked up the phone yet again.

"Yeah?" Bill answered the phone.

"Ah. Yeah. Hi. Can you make . . ." I glanced at my notes from my phone call with Mac in which he spouted all the specs. "Solid-shank, cold-forged, truss-head CDA 110 electrolytic copper rivets?"

"Sure."

I wanted to jump out of my chair but waited. "Like, do you have the wire in stock? Right now?"

"Yup. Lots of it." Bill was clearly a northern Wisconsinite through and through.

"Um. How many can you make? Thousands?"

"Sure."

I finally gave in to the excitement and let it spill. "This is awesome! Seriously, we've been trying to find someone like you! Can I have my buddy call you to discuss and put in an order?"

"Oh, sure."

"How do I put in an order? Email?"

"Aw, nah, I don't fire that sonofabitch up. You need me, you fax."

Immediately after I hung up with Bill, I called Mac and gave him the good news.

Last, it was time to find someone willing to hand-wipe tin in the interior of the copper pots. Historically, copper was lined with tin, which was what I wanted to do, too. Mac and I knew of one tinner, Dan, in Ohio who could do an amazing job, but we also knew that if both of us put in orders of more than fifty pieces each, we'd have a big bottleneck. I needed to find other possibilities.

Wanting to cover all my options, I dug around for different ideas just to be sure I wasn't missing anything or anyone in the lining choices. I debated, briefly, putting thin-dense hard chrome (TDHC) on the interior, hoping it would be a happy medium between stainless steel and tin. On long car rides, I called and spoke with a retired metallurgist in Texas about how this might be a viable copper pot interior. He said etching the copper with acid to create "nanostructures" for the chrome to attach to, like Velcro on a microscopic level, should work, since the two metals wouldn't bond on a molecular level.

Armed with that particular knowledge, I started the next round of calls. TDHC is a proprietary material, so there were only a few people who could have applied it for me. Top that off with the fact that TDHC was created to be sprayed on industrial items or motorcycles—no one knew if it would work on cookware. No one had lined cookware with chrome before, let alone TDHC. Would it stick? Chip? Was it really food safe? How would it look? Cook? (By the time I'd reached this stage, the guys I spoke to wondered if I was an engineer. I'm still not sure if they believed me when I said, "No, I'm a wedding planner! But I want to make cookware. . . .") After con-

I picked tin lining for my cookware line and then, yup, started to apply it myself. In the garage.

vincing the guys to try some samples of the TDHC on the copper, I didn't like the look and frankly had no idea if this would fly in terms of cookware use. It also wasn't part of the traditional cookware I'd researched in the very beginning, and so ultimately I discarded TDHC as a lining option.

Eventually, Dan took the tinning work to line the inside, and Mac and I resigned ourselves to the fact that we'd just have to dance around each other during the holidays and hope we didn't get too backed up. We both assumed orders would hit a high during the holiday season; that model has proven correct for me and I'm pretty sure for Mac as well. That fourth quarter really helps us have enough funds to buy more copper for the following year!

The manufacturers and fabricators now had all the pieces to make my American copper cookware, but I was still only an observer. For over a year, I had others making every piece of the copper cookware for me, and I was selling it only after it was completely manufactured by other hands. I didn't have the copper forming under my fingers or the molten tin sloshing around my gloves. The rivets were not hammered in by my own machinery, and I certainly didn't have a way to make each copper pot shine. I was researching, sketching, and approving designs and processes for my cookware—whether copper, iron, or clay—but not actually making it. Still, though I didn't have the hands-on knowledge to make these items myself, it was exciting to see my napkin sketches brought to life. The slow, careful research about traditional cookware shapes, sizes, and materials I'd done was becoming grounded in reality. Working with makers who would build pans to my designs and pots to my specifications was vindicating and exhilarating.

I thought back to that girl I was who had burned her finger at seventeen. And I wanted to learn more—to someday make my cookware line myself.

In case it isn't clear, I like to research. Sitting in my office, with white, watery light spilling through the rectangles of my windows, I was searching for details yet again on how cookware really was made back in the 1800s. Thanks to Google, an old newspaper clipping came to the top, praising the artisanal capabilities of a master tinsmith (who also did copper work) located north of me, in West Bend, Wisconsin.

That man was Bob Bartelme of Backwoods Tin & Copper, and he was kind and welcoming on the phone. He said I could certainly pop up and visit, but no, I couldn't bring my young children, and yes, an afternoon would work. So I lined up a sitter and trailed up the country roads.

Bob and Marilyn, his wife of over fifty years, live in the country on a retired hobby farm where he uses the barns for his shop and tool storage. Driving past his property the first time by accident, I saw multiple copper and tin lanterns lining the posts of his driveway. His trade couldn't be more obvious.

Bob ushered me into his tin shop, a detached, two-stall garage that's been completely taken over by the tools of the trade. The floors are stained cement, the windows squat and smudged, and half the lights are wide tin lanterns made by Bob but outfitted with electricity. The outside light glows gold, dancing on all the machine dust floating through the air, and the ever-present shadows in the corners would be populated by spiders if they could stand the soot. It's organized only in that Bob knows where everything is, and I quickly learned that Bob owns almost every tool imaginable. They're cobbled together in vintage wooden drawers, hanging from walls, hidden under tables, and stored in a jumbled menagerie of engine parts. It's both astounding and overwhelming. He has a shelf along the longest wall of the garage peppered with nails, each nail holding flat patterns for the tinware he makes, labeled with his broad, capitalized script: BETTY LAMP or RUSSIAN MESS KIT or HALF MOON CANTEEN or FIFE CASE.

Bob is a retired mechanic. He has decades of hands-on knowledge from building Harley-Davidson motorcycles from scratch, programing CNC metal-spinning machines, and fixing engines. A tradesman his whole life, he has learned by doing, and no school could teach the depth of what he knows. His wavy, silver-and-gray hair and beard were once fiery red, he's a couple of inches taller than my five foot three inches, and he gravitates to wearing suspenders paired with worn jeans or overalls and a well-loved Harley-themed T-shirt. Bob's pushing seventy but acts (and can wield tools) as if he's barely fifty.

That first day, over the course of several hours, Bob dropped his current project to give me a tutorial on how he made a tin mug. I was entranced

Robert "Bob" Bartelme, master tinsmith

Bob's tin shop, West Bend, Wisconsin

and completely overwhelmed with the geometry and mathematics that went into making even a simple cup. Still, when I was leaving, Bob said casually, "Next time, why don't you make a cup?" Absolutely I'd come back and try my hand at creating a piece of usable, vintage reproduction cookware! And the next time I visited his shop, I did. I think that cup took me more than six hours.

Tin sheet metal is actually a thin piece of steel that's been electroplated with tin (in the old days, metalworkers would dip sheets of steel into vats of molten tin, which we now call hot-dip tin); this is done to keep the steel from rusting. Just to cut the pieces required the use of hundred-year-old tools. There was so much to absorb: the names of the machines (grooving, wiring, setting down), how to avoid scratching the tin, how to solder the seams and check for leaks, how to etch my name in the bottom. To prepare the pieces, I used stomp shears, which require one to cut the metal by literally stomping on a huge foot bar, and a touchy, long tool called a circle cutter, which did exactly that—it cut the circle for the cup base.

These old machines were all black and oiled to working perfection, and

Patterns in Bob's shop, ready for building reproduction tinware
Right: The first tin mug I ever made. Now, years later, I've made more than I can count!

I fluctuated between concern that I'd break an antique tool from 1820 and fear that I'd hurt a finger. Bob stood next to me, demonstrating his methods and grabbing up different pieces before I could ruin them. When I put on his old, battered leather glove and tried to create a burr (a ninety-degree angle in the metal), I failed repeatedly. Bob chuckled and explained that using the burring machine was about the hardest part of learning the tinsmithing trade.

As we finished, Bob grinned and off-handedly remarked, "Next time, why don't you try something in copper?"

And I thought, *Hell, yeah! Copper! That's what I'm talking about!*

Over the next months, I drove up to Bob's shop at least once but usually twice a week. In the beginning, he was doing what he did that first day: letting me build something relatively easy for myself. After two months, I was helping him make items for his never-ending list of customer orders. Suddenly Bob was introducing me to his acquaintances as his apprentice, and I realized I was just that. My kids started to come to the shop once Bob and I realized they could be trusted to not touch the dangerous tools. Sometimes people ask me why I didn't keep the kids away, but truthfully, I love that they now are respectful of and comfortable around hot irons, fire, and rolling machines.

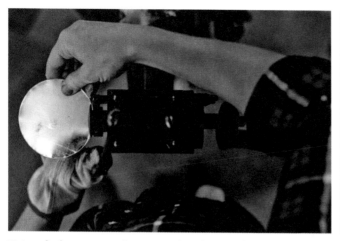 

Using the burring machine to make a bottom for a tin mug
Right: Me, Bob, and copper pots. A typical arrangement.

By this point, I'd sold my event-planning company. My heart was no longer burning with excitement when choosing centerpiece designs or invitation fonts; I'd found a different creative trade that felt solid, real, and physically powerful. I traded brides for band saws. Now I was bending metal and using tools from the 1800s, forgetting my wedding ring at the shop when I'd leave it on the side of the bench, getting grease in the creases of my fingers, and learning how to do impossible fractions (how do you add a $^{15}/_{32}$ burr to a circle of copper sheet?).

Bob has had a profound influence on my life. And it's not just because my kids call him and his wife Grandpa and Grandma. He's taught me so much about the old trades and crafts that I am both amazed at his constant flow of knowledge and scared I won't remember half of it, and the information will continue its slow leak away from American awareness. How many tinsmiths do you know? How many coppersmiths? If you can name more than a few, you're in the minority. Until I started working with copper and iron, I knew zero people doing any of these crafts and keeping the old trades alive. It used to be that everyone knew someone, and that was only a few decades ago.

I don't want our American traditions and trades to become more and more obscure until they die. If we have to go to other countries to find pieces to build cookware, or if no one is left to carry on the knowledge, we've lost more than just a trade. A manufacturer in China may be able to stamp out replicas based on some photographs, but we will have lost part of our history.

How do we revitalize these trades? How do we keep the knowledge alive and well? I have faith in upcoming generations to help. Think of all those craft beers spilling onto the shelves in grocery stores, or people raising a few chickens (guilty!), or the cheesemakers (I sense a definite Wisconsin theme now...), or people leaving the cities to take up hobby or sustenance farming.

Even on my own in the garage, I learn something each and every time I put fire and flame to copper. It's exciting and challenging to save these dying trades, and as a woman coming into a man's world, I have fresh eyes. I get to ask "Why not?"

Well, I'm a woman who writes, so this book is my small part in celebrating and preserving this history. And there are so many other people out there—men *and* women—who are creative and drawn to this deeply tactile way of living that I can only hope some of the words here will inspire others to ask questions, dive in, and get their hands dirty.

I still go to Bob's every week, with the kids eagerly joining me. They like to bend scrap pieces into strange shapes or bang on tinner's stakes, of which Bob has a plethora in different shapes. Like a blacksmith's anvil but made of softer metal, the stakes are where we hammer and shape the sheet of glimmering tin and copper to suit the patterns of cookware pieces.

My youngest child, Jack, has been with me the most during school days, and when Bob and I pose as tinsmiths for historical reenactments, Jack isn't shy about engaging the public with his own smithing knowledge.

"See this hammer?" he asks passersby, demonstrating by whacking on a tool dating back to the 1760s. "It hams. See me hamming? Forty dollars."

At those reenactments of my own youth, where my siblings and I wandered under the pines and falling leaves in the Wisconsin summers and autumns, I felt an indescribable delight in trailing from cooper to candlemaker to fur trader. There were so many children in the camps running around in leather and calico, but we could only watch or participate in carefully regulated crafts. I remember seeing two teenage girls in the river,

Bob teaching my son Will how to swing a swedge, which is an original tool made in the mid-1700s that we still use!

their skirts bundled around their waists, washing their hair in the shallows to cool off from the summer heat. They were laughing and glowing golden in the afternoon light. The trees climbing the banks behind them were black, but the river was almost white with reflected sun, and the tiny insects and cottonwood fluff turning in the air made me feel, just for a moment and quite viscerally, that I'd fallen backward in time. I knew, even as an eight-year-old, that someday I wanted to be just like those girls.

Funny enough, that same northern Wisconsin reenactment still happens some thirty-odd years later. I love falling back into 1820, when the world was simpler, fires needed constant watching, and work was never done. My children get to spend three hours at the knee of a man willing to show them flint knapping and how to spin a rope from the dried strands of stinging nettle. I have Bob to thank for this hobby, too.

We spend days interacting in a park with children and their families, teaching them the old trade of a tinsmith and coppersmith. The eagerness in their bright round-cheeked faces is heartening. You can tell if they had a choice that they'd camp with us all weekend. They desperately want to take up the hammer and bang on the tin sheet. They want to put on the old clothes and live in a tent all night long. And I can't say I blame them, because I was once just like them—watching and wishing.

My own children get what I didn't because my family never dressed up or camped: a chance to live like the old fur traders, under gigantic canopies of maples and oaks, carrying lanterns filled with candlelight at night, whittling away at sticks to make spears or chopping wood with a miniature tomahawk. I love how the nights are filled with dew, fire, and the sounds of old-fashioned music and song; how clay jugs of homemade brew are passed casually; how I get to wear layers of petticoats; and how I have learned to fight the coals so I don't burn a pie buried in a Dutch oven. So I reenact and attend traditional fur-trade rendezvous to work with the youth, to give my children memories no one can steal, and to satisfy that little girl in me who immortalized those teens bathing in a Wisconsin river.

Washing dishes the super old-fashioned way

Jack and Hannah drinking out of homemade tin mugs. They weren't pretty, but at least they didn't leak!

What can I say about Bob? My ongoing apprenticeship with him is filled with teasing, stories, and hands-on learning. We work to create patterns from scratch together, figuring it out as we go. He never makes me feel stupid, even though with some basic mechanical things, I totally am. In fact, he's family, as is his entire family. We go to their house for Christmas dinner and weddings, and Bob and his wife, Marilyn, are the emergency contacts on my kids' school forms. Bob is the salt of the earth, generosity personified. Because let's be real, it takes a lot of patience to teach. But he did. He gave me the confidence to do this trade. Bob is the reason I am coppersmith.

What is the hardest thing about keeping the old trades alive?

It's finding people who want to do the trade and learn the craft—that's the hardest part. It's also tricky to find the market, the people willing and interested in buying not only vintage pieces but handmade ones. And it's very hard to make a real living doing this line of work, so it's been moved to a type of hobby instead of a trade.

How were tinsmiths different from coppersmiths?

Originally, coppersmiths really focused only on making stills and fishpans. That was back in the 1700s, when every house had one of each of those items. Everyone made their own beer and, if they were wealthy, their own whiskey, and needed the stills. So a coppersmith was either making them or repairing them. The tinsmith made basic kitchenware for everyone—for preparing, cooking, and serving food—as well as doing the repairs on everything. It was easier and cheaper to use tinware for everything instead of even cast iron at the time, and the repairs were inexpensive, too.

In the 1800s, when machines for making sheet metal came around, coppersmiths started to move into working on the exteriors of homes. At that time, roofs, cornices, and gutters were usually made of copper, and all the scuppers for rain gutters were, too. Tinsmiths slowly became today's sheet metal workers, and now you'll find them as your duct workers, or people who install heating, ventilation, and air-conditioning systems.

Were all copper (and tin) wares thin or thick in the early years?

They were pretty thin until the 1850s, when stamping machinery became available. Then it was possible to use thicker gauges [sheets] of copper. The ability to stamp and form sheet metal with machines changed the whole industry.

Which was used more often—tin or copper cookware?

It depended on whether a family was rich or poor. Plus, tin was considered "disposable." Eventually it would wear down from continual use on cast-iron stoves, or it would rust. A lot of tin artifacts have rusted, whereas copper won't. In the late 1800s, the people in Williamsburg, Virginia, would just toss old tin items into wells, it was considered so disposable.

A January backyard seasoning party, complete with ice on the ground and beer buried in the snow nearby

Bob's faith in me was the reason I even considered bringing the majority of my copper cookware manufacturing in-house, which meant finding power tools and working in my garage all year. Before that, I'd only seasoned my cast-iron skillets at home over big fires in old giant metal cylinders (burn barrels). And the only reason I was so hands-on about firing the skillets was that it was frankly not feasible to find someone to season the skillets for me (the cost of shipping those heavy pans alone would have done me in)! Seasoning was about the extent of my hands-on approach. Whether it was over ice and snow (with a beer in hand) or in the summer (also with a beer), we'd fire up those burn barrels to at least 600°F and watch the raw cast-iron skillets turn black from the glittery, sparkling silver of fresh cast iron. I thought hand seasoning over fire was pretty good for an unseasoned metalsmith.

But with Bob's tutelage and his knowledge and ability to make a jig (a piece of wood or iron used as a pattern to reproduce a custom design so that we can make multiples of an item without having to constantly remeasure), and with help from the guys at the foundry in Ohio, who would spin the copper cookware pot bodies, and the small ductile iron foundry in Lodi, California, which provided the handles for the copperware, suddenly making the copper cookware myself was possible.

After a year of working with Bob as his apprentice, I bounced in one morning and poured myself a cup of his ever-available coffee.

"Hey, do you think I could drill the handles and attach them myself to the copper pots?" I asked.

Bob looked at me. "Well, sure."

"And I could tin the inside. We did it that one time at the convergence...."

He nodded. "You could."

Relief poured through me, but I wasn't done asking. "But can you help me?"

"Sure. We have to make some jigs," he said, shrugging like making jigs was no big deal, speaking with just the right amount of amusement and support in his tone. "There will be a lot of trial and error."

I waved my hand. "I don't care! Let's do it!"

And soon after this conversation, Bob took me to buy an air compressor and appropriate rivet gun and air hose.

The annual tinsmith convergence (which always has a few coppersmiths as well as a handful of blacksmiths and tinkers) is open to all, and especially those who work with sheet metal specifically in the way of historical trades. We trade knowledge, expertise, findings, and experiments and swap tools. There are discussions on how to make a cookware pattern just by looking at a historical item and workshop seminars where everyone gets to try their hand at creating their own hot-dip tin sheets, for example. Always there are used books on the trade from the early colonial times for sale. Sometimes women bring their spinning wheels and make thread or yarn; others will design holiday ornaments from pieces of cut tin. Some of the guys talk about how to fix the old machines, or repaint them, or how to sharpen the old tin snips (fancy but strong scissors). Most years, a man versus machine race is held to see who can most quickly make a tin cup that doesn't leak—the guy doing everything with hand pliers or the guy using 1800s rotary machines (like that tricky burring machine). I have gone with my husband and kids in tow, who may or may not be absorbing knowledge just by osmosis, and other times by myself.

Every year, I get to fend off constant good-natured ribbing and teasing and ask a thousand questions of very smart craftsmen. The guys support my venture into the trade, but they don't say, "We're so excited you're picking up tinsmithing, Sara!" They say, with a twinkle in their eye, "You finally showed up today. You sleep in?" It's a wonderful time, and the amount of oral history exchanged is priceless. The best part, though, is learning something new and useful, which has since translated into my ability to actually make cookware in my garage.

One of the most important parts of tool gathering was finding the items needed to hand-wipe the tin interiors onto the copper pots. The first time I tried to tin copper I was at one of the tinsmith convergences. Sitting on grass under large trees, with a small audience of old tinsmiths and some of their wives, I watched Dan a few times before trying the process myself.

Tinning involves holding a copper piece over a fire until it gets hot everywhere, then putting on a flux, the essential fluid that helps bond the tin to the copper. When the flux is nice and ready, you add tin, which stays liquid as you hold the copper over the fire. The tin must be wiped around with your free hand, with any excess tipped or wiped off. The cookware is then slowly immersed in warm water to set. Needless to say, the amount of tools, fire, and safety equipment to do this process is pretty extensive!

An uncounted number of tools later, and a garage full of buffing (polishing) wheel dust, grime, and tin shavings—a totally *not* child-proof space—I was building cookware in the cave where the car belongs but no longer fits. Now I regularly burn my hands, just like when I spent time in Uncle Doug's forge. In fact, as I write this right now, one finger is sore because last night I accidentally put it in front of a blowtorch while working on tinning some vintage copper.

A new copper skillet getting its first-ever coat of tin!

The garage, sans cars, is where
I tin the copper in the winter.
FYI: This photo does not show all
the proper equipment. I usually
wear a welding cap, a full-face
mask, and a carbon air canister!

Sometimes I mess up royally. I lose my grip on a copper pot while cleaning it, and it spins away and warps beyond repair. I still need to build a real tinner's bench for hand-wiping the tin inside the pots, so I don't have to crouch over a fire in my driveway. The ductile iron handles of the copper cookware can give me grief if they get wet before I grind, sand, and drill them to rivet them onto the copper pot bodies, and then they rust, so the handles turn reddish and I have to clean them off again. I never have enough time to season cast-iron skillets, and I keep waiting for the day one of the kids will accidentally ride a bike into a fire.

Every single day I go into the shop, I get hurt. I ruin something. I swear at one of the two-hundred-year-old machines, which were bought from the tinsmith convergence's tool swap, or from eBay, or even traded from Bob. I spill flux, forget to put on my breathing mask, and come up with new ideas I have no clue how to execute. As time has passed, I have received more and more retinning and restoration work, which requires a ton of physical hard labor. If I don't get to Bob's every week, I feel disjointed and have to almost relearn the touch and delicacy of the burring machine all over again.

I often stare at the copper restoration projects that people send me and I think they're going to be next to impossible, especially the three-hundred-year-old coffeepots with three-inch holes that were previously repaired with now-rusted tin patches, and the teakettles that were boiled dry until their spouts fell off, and the old stockpots that are so huge and heavy I'm quite sure they won't fit on my tools! You know that feeling when you're your own worst critic? Yeah, imagine that feeling, coupled with the fact that I still have so much to learn.

It was never my intention to become a coppersmith and fill my garage with old vintage hand-turning machines and power tools. Shop classes in high school were mystical electives that felt so out of my reach I never stepped foot in that classroom. I didn't understand how the guys who walked out couldn't get the blacking from their hands. Every day I'm using the subjects that were (and still are) the hardest for me to conquer—math, chemistry, and mechanics. Now I'm the one with creases in my fingers that are never quite clean.

But I'm also still able to be creative. Getting my hands in the thick of it makes me appreciate anything handcrafted in a way I never did as a kid in art class. It's visceral. If you want to really understand how a copper pot is put together, go to a folk school and spend a day touching the metal and smashing a hammer. If your interests lean more toward textile arts, take a weaving class. Go out and ask questions of those people hidden in the corners of the world, quietly keeping their trade alive.

This book is about copper, iron, and clay—the traditional cookware found in homes—but I don't claim that I personally make each piece! It's been a wonderful part of the journey to discover the makers, experts, and artisans in each of these fields who offer their joy and enthusiasm as they re-create kitchenware and share it in these pages. This is a celebration of the real cookware found in homes across the world and across the ages, made from the three basic materials that are the building blocks of our kitchens.

The challenge of creating these pieces is exhilarating. The sense of confidence when I finish a piece bleeds into my daily life and creates this strong sensation of conquering the world, even if it's just a small victory within the walls of my garage. The constant education is addicting and the sharing of knowledge from artisans never, ever gets old. If I could, I'd have you all come over and hang out in the shop and do as much hands-on cookware building as you'd like. You'd learn along with me. We'd exchange trivia about pans and pots and food. But until an airport gets built here, this book is as good as it gets.

So, did you know . . .

Using the stomp shears to cut copper sheet. No makeup artist—that is accidental but real soot on my face.

COPPER

Copper has been used for thousands of years, and I am totally obsessed with the history of how it came to be in our kitchens. While I may give lots of exciting trivia information here and go through the high points of the past, I'll also dive into the different kinds of copper cookware made around the world and explain the mystery of how and why copper works the way it does when you cook with it. I'll give general care, use, and cleaning instructions, too, and you'll finish this chapter equipped with a solid understanding about copper cookware. Then you can have a dinner party and share what I hope is bountiful excitement about copper!

See this pot? It is one of the two that my husband ran over with the car—casualties of a garage copper shop. This pot Bob and I repaired so only a few wrinkles show. The other pot? We burned a hole in it when trying to fix it.

THE HISTORY OF COPPER

Copper and people have an exceptionally long, even *romantic* relationship. At some point between sixty-five hundred and eight thousand years ago, copper made a colorful debut—colorful because the metal catapulted the human race out of the Stone Age. Copper tools were the very first metal tools used by people, and the metallurgical techniques used to refine copper emerged in several locations simultaneously. Sumerians and Chaldeans, who lived in Mesopotamia (an area that today includes Kuwait, Iraq, Syria, Jordan, Lebanon, and Israel), began to smelt copper for various purposes. This means that copper was, as far as archaeologists and anthropologists can tell, the first and only usable metal known to humans for more than five thousand years.

Items made from copper last a long time, which is why archaeologists keep finding copper items in exploratory digs in the Middle East. I dream the same will happen to the copper cookware I build in my garage! Copper doesn't rust, so it shouldn't ever need to be discarded. If plain, or lined with tin as vintage pieces are, and kept up, it should last lifetimes upon lifetimes—no landfill required. In contrast, cookware with iron in it, which includes stainless steel, may eventually fall apart over time. It's why we find whole copper and bronze ewers that are thousands of years old; in contrast, iron cooking pots less than nine hundred years old usually rust into tiny fragments.

Once those ancient smiths became well acquainted with soft copper, it was likely a happy accident that led to the creation of stronger metals. Ancient copper was combined with arsenic, which created a hard, durable metal that was preferable to traditional stone for tools and weapons (of course all brainpower went to weapons first and kitchen tools afterward). Copper was often used for small items, such as hooks, awls, spearheads, and chisels, but pots and trays have also been found in excavations.

Eventually, copper fabrication practices spread to neighboring Egypt, which kept the smithing alive after Sumer and Chaldea collapsed. Thanks to those ancient Egyptians, metalworking in copper became a cornerstone of Western civilization. The Egyptians fell in love with copper and used a ridiculous amount of it. It was a staple for cooking pots, bowls, and small implements in homes, such as knives. Those born into wealthy families used copper vessels to carry and store water, which killed most bacteria from tainted water sources; the Egyptians seemed to know about copper's health-promoting qualities well before science could explain them. And I wonder sometimes whether our ancestors understood the conductive properties of copper. Did they notice how well the copper conducted heat? How fast and uniformly the fire's energy spread up the sides? Or did they take it for granted, as it was the only metal cookware available at the time?

Those brilliant Egyptian smiths are generally credited with the adding of tin to copper to make the alloy bronze. But Egypt's domestic copper mines were insufficient to meet demand for this metal. Significant quantities of ore were imported from Syria and the western reaches of Asia as early as 2600 BCE.

Copper kitchenware found in Egyptian digs was formed by hammering, or "planishing," as the technique is known, with the spouts and handles joined using copper rivets. The crazy part is that's pretty much how we still assemble copperware today in the metal shop. Time has stood still in some respects, as has the craftsmanship and heirloom quality. That's what makes something truly valuable—to know that it is reusable and renewable forever with just a bit of TLC.

When iron replaced copper for military use, people began to adopt copper for other applications. Roman architects designed buildings with copper plumbing, and Roman smiths used molds to create copper kitchen items and cookware. It was still a bit pricey back then, and larger pieces of cookware, such as cauldrons, were most likely owned by more prosperous people.

Cleopatra's Countless Kitchens

My Brooklyn friend Mac once told me a story about Cleopatra and her banquets. He said it was rumored that Cleopatra's palace in Alexandria had twelve kitchens, each of which contained the exact same number and size of pots and pans and serving vessels (probably some of them copper!). During a banquet, each kitchen would prepare the exact same food, thirty minutes after the one ahead of it. This was supposed to accommodate orators (Cleopatra likely had a lot of long-winded Roman guests) who should not be interrupted by the arrival of all the food. To ensure the banquet meal was presented perfectly at the right temperature, if the orator wasn't finished by the time the first kitchen was ready, the food would be tossed, and the next kitchen would prepare to serve the meal. On it went, every thirty minutes or so, until the orator finally shut up. Can you imagine? And we moan about waste!

Romans enjoyed ready access to copper deposits across their empire, and they also had an extensive system of improved roads (and countless slaves) to move those raw materials. We find evidence of copper cauldrons, buckets, water, storage jugs, and servingware in various Roman excavations. As far back as the sixth century BCE, ornate but narrowly purposed wine buckets called *oinochoai* (jugs reserved for pouring during entertaining and not much else) were a common fixture in many households. Macedonian archaeological digs have unveiled more bronze kitchenware, such as ladles, strainers, and vessels made solely for foot washing. Copper was used almost everywhere.

The Chinese were developing their own copper technology, too, separate from what was happening in the West, though there is always a chance some traveler brought the knowledge from one group to another. Copper in China was usually used with tin, though, and the Chinese had all kinds of recipes for making different items. For instance, to make cauldrons, you needed five parts copper to one part tin. Each type of shape had its own metallic makeup, and this system was much more precise than what was happening in the Middle East and Europe.

How Did They Do That?
Making Copper Cookware in Ancient Times

In antiquity, copper had been cast—meaning poured as liquid metal into molds—as small parts to be joined to thin but larger fabricated or planished bodies. Early copper vessels started as "cores" made of clay. Wax was sculpted and applied over the core in strips. The completed piece would have the exact shape, thickness, and measurement of the intended vessel in wax with the clay core below it, including detailing such as legs or handles. When the artisan was satisfied, the wax would be covered in clay and left to dry.

While drying, the components would generally shrink. To keep the core, wax, and outer clay layer properly aligned, workers would pass a rod from the bottom up through all three materials. Once the metal was ready to cast, the mold was heated, the wax poured out, and the prepared molten metal poured in, usually through the hole in the bottom left by the rod, which acted as the "gate" for the metal. After the metal cooled, one would need to break the mold (hence the old saying!) to remove the cast metal. The smith would then plug the rod hole in the bottom with filler metal.

Molds used to cast copper or bronze objects are referred to as patterns now, so when I say "pattern" or even "match plate," that's what I mean. Patterns allow for repetition, which makes smithing more efficient and fast. Reusable patterns meant that metalsmiths could create items faster and in more precise shapes rather than simply banging metal around the corner of a stone or tool. This in turn meant that metal items that were previously considered luxuries became steadily less expensive.

Copper and bronze pots prior to the 1800s were often created using traditional pottery shapes as a guide, though the "lost wax" process described above could also be used to create art and statues.

Centuries passed, artisanship flourished, and functional and decorative metal items began to be found in homes all over Europe.

In Denmark, copper was used interchangeably with iron in tenth-century kitchens. Copper was also widely used in the Danes' famed textile businesses: huge five-gallon sheet copper pots have been found in medieval dye houses. Besides iron and soapstone, copper alloy pots have been discovered in early Nordic homes. They were not large—only 2 to 3 gallons in capacity and up to 14 inches in diameter—but this shows the breadth of copper cookware usage. Copper was coveted, respected, and treated as an heirloom even in the beginning. But while metal cookware use expanded greatly from the tenth century on, the plague thwarted economic growth, and copper cookware didn't return to the pages of the historical record until the Renaissance.

During the Renaissance, sophisticated cooks (those people working in the kitchens of the nobility) possessed an array of tools beyond knives and cauldrons. They had long-handled frying pans, waffle irons, cleavers, tongs, scales, skimming spoons, and cheese graters. Most were made of classic cooking metals: copper as pure copper or a bronze mix, or iron.

Soon copper cookware became commonplace in the kitchens of the nobility, so castles often boasted a dizzying array of copper in various states of blackening from age and use. For instance, estates like Hampton Court in Richmond, England, had a separate boiling house where huge copper cauldrons set directly inside chimneys were in constant use to make porridge, soups, and broths.

Eventually, access to copper kitchen tools began working its way down the class ladder to the houses of courtiers and merchants. By the 1600s, copper was becoming a staple in average kitchens, and French chefs created the craze for a well-equipped kitchen filled with proper tools.

When workers or peasants wanted a copper pot but could not afford a fully shaped or a completely new one, they usually could find one that someone had pieced together from scraps. Lads working in the smelting foundries would save the copper "clinkers" (scraps) that came out of the furnaces during the milling process. Once they had enough copper, they'd hammer out the malleable metal into haphazard thin sheets and then solder and rivet the pieces together. The finished products were known as "clinker pots," and they provided a taste of luxury to poorer people.

Did You Know? Illegal Colonial Copper

Fun fact: Only small sheets of copper were available to the smiths in colonial America—another rule imposed by the Crown—so making larger
cookware items always involved piecing copper sheets together. The colonists mined copper in New England, shipped it to England for smelting
and making into sheets, and then paid to have it shipped back. No wonder the colonists said, "To hell with that—we'll smelt and roll it here and
not tell the British." That totally happened.

Colonial copper shapes,
made "in the flat" by hand

From the 1700s on, particularly in Europe and in wealthier colonial American homes, copper was a fixture in enough kitchens to stimulate the design and manufacture of new styles of pots, kettles, cauldrons, and utensils, but the thin copper sheets they used has meant that you won't find many pots from the old days with a thickness of 1.5 mm or 3 mm (that thickness is more the standard today). Thick sheets would break the expensive hand-crank machines the smith spent months saving up to buy. While still able to conduct heat wonderfully, thinner walls resulted in soft goods that bent, popped, dented, or leaked relatively quickly. The benefit was that this cookware could be fixed easily by a tinker, adding to the cookware's long life and making the items less expensive in the long run. Even two hundred years later, I can take a copper pot that doesn't sit "true" or flat, heat it, and softly, slowly hammer the bottom or side back to the proper shape. Tinkering as a trade isn't completely dead.

Tinsmiths and coppersmiths were usually interchangeable in their ability to manufacture metal pieces for the kitchen. Technically, tinsmiths work with tin sheet and coppersmiths work with copper sheet, but a competent sheet metal smith can work with both. When a tinker came to town, he could repair any tin or copper piece needing work, as both were formed using the same methods and tools.

As technology evolved, so did the ability to form copper pots. Soon smiths could have pieces pressed by the Dover Stamping Company (in New Hampshire) or another large company and no longer needed to create cookware from scratch. Efficiency meant cheaper cookware for the average family to buy and own. The most recognizable piece of the period was also one of the easiest to make: the copper frying pan. I'm a huge fan of this particular versatile piece of copper cookware, and I designed one that is the centerpiece of my House Copper collection.

COPPER COOKWARE CREATION BEFORE ELECTRICITY

Coppersmiths did a roaring trade until the end of the 1800s. Before the Industrial Revolution took root, copper cookware was made in a cottage industry of artisans who passed along the trade orally and with multiyear apprenticeships. Everything was done by hand using hand tools and tinner's anvil stakes. If you were alive in 1820 and lived in a big enough town

Copper seams come in four different shapes: lap, crimp, cramp/dovetail, and double bottom. One piece can have several: This one has a crimp seam along the sides and a double-bottom seam on the bottom. The pot sitting on the counter has a cramp seam on the base.

and you wanted a copper pot, you'd walk down the road and tell your local smith what you'd like. The master coppersmith would bend, roll, or form a sheet of copper according to the pattern he used for a piece of cookware. If the item was to be large, several sheets of copper would be connected with copper rivets (little nails, essentially). The copper would be notched along the corners and then edges prepared for a seam. Once the cookware had its basic shape, the smith would measure the bottom, cut, burr, and join it to the main body and then solder everything together with tin by using a ridiculous amount of heat to create a leakproof cookware vessel. If necessary, the coppersmith would send the ware off to the tinner to be tinned on the inside, or he'd do it himself if he doubled as both tinsmith and coppersmith. Hardware handles could be added, made from copper or brass, or iron from the local blacksmith.

When copper cookware was made by hand, it was made to last. Why do you think it's still possible to find a functioning copper boiler from the Revolutionary War era or earlier? That was heirloom manufacturing at its finest.

Every week, I get to pretend I live two hundred years ago and pull out tin snips; crank on handles to create burrs; fold metal into lap, crimp, double-bottom, or cramp seams; and solder pieces together with tin using either a modern soldering iron or vintage coppers (old-fashioned soldering irons) to make cookware.

By the mid-1800s, most smiths were able to afford machines created specifically for the tin and coppersmith trade, which allowed for cookware to be made quickly and more uniformly (and cheaply!). Copper cookware was well on its way to being mass produced. Cookware creation became the realm of large fabricators—factories that could support the mechanical processes needed to make lots of pieces really fast for higher profits. As people were swept away by these huge industrial leaps, the craftsmanship of pure copper cookware was lost to speed, resulting in ultimately often poorly made (though cheaper!) products.

BUILDING TIN-LINED COPPER FROM SCRATCH

Apart from the tin-lining application, copper cookware construction is similar to any other basic metal manufacturing process. But since we're discussing my (and hopefully your) love affair with cookware, we may as well dive into the quick version of cookware building. I want to give a clear picture of what it takes to make that pot you put on your stove, whether it's made by a machine, another artisan, or yours truly.

Norbert Overla, the engineering manager at Ohio Metal, thinks copper is one of the hardest things to manufacture. In his words, "the cons out-weigh the pros" when it comes to actually handling the metal. Part of that is the incredible heat generated so quickly by copper, even in the making of copper pot bodies.

"Just try and saw a copper rivet to a shorter length," Norb explains. "The heat generated from the friction of the saw will blister your fingers."

But even with the difficulties in creating copper pots and pans, Norb himself will agree that true copper cookware is "a onetime purchase that will last a lifetime and then some."

When I put in an order for some copper pot components, it sets off a chain reaction. The copper starts in the form of raw material. During the smelting, heating, and refining of the copper, oxygen is removed from it using different elements, such as phosphorous. The copper is then pressed into sheets of different thicknesses, which are sent to a fabricator who cuts round discs out of the sheet according to the design order. The disks are placed on a stainless-steel or wooden tool that is shaped like the interior of the desired copper cookware and locked inside a CNC automated milling machine. When the machine is spinning, an arm draws the copper disk up around the tool and forms the cooking pot, pan, or bowl. Voilà! That's the body component.

Meanwhile, using a similar milling process, the iron or brass foundry is busy making match plates and handles for the cookware. The molten metal is poured into the sand casts made by the match plate. After it cools, it's cleaned, excess metal is ground off on a grinding wheel, and it's shipped off to be connected to the copper pot body.

At this point, semitrucks pull up to my driveway to drop off heavy pallets. So far my neighbors haven't complained, but I feel conspicuous every time. These pallets contain the blank copper bodies and fresh iron handles. I'll grind, clean, sand, measure, and drill the handles and copper bodies. Using a rivet gun with a specially made insert (thanks to Bob the master smith, once again) and a support system that sits on my tinner's anvil, I hammer in copper rivets to connect the handles. Then it's time to heat the cookware over flame and apply the tin interiors by hand-wiping. That's an art, too! (It's what I'm shown doing on the cover of this book.) When the pans cool, it's time to clean, buff, and polish them before sending them off to a customer.

Many people ask about the tin lining in my cookware—and in vintage cookware, too. They ask what the metal is, how it works, and why it's there. First and foremost, copper cookware must be lined with something to keep the heated copper from leaching into your food, and tin is my choice (I'll talk about overall lining options in a bit). Tin is a micronutrient and a necessary part of our diet, but it also makes the cookware food safe. A tin lining is relatively nonreactive and allows for cooking pretty much everything and anything in the pot, even acidic foods like tomato sauce. Tin is also the historically accurate choice, one that feeds my personal philosophy about going back to the basics of a pioneer kitchen. Not to mention that it's something I can actually apply as a small-shop coppersmith!

The pieces I make now are replicas of original heirlooms. They act and

Tinning and then buffing a copper skillet

look exactly like they did back in the day. Making copper cookware is almost too much fun, but it certainly makes me appreciate the amount of work that was required to build each piece of cookware in, say, 1790.

It's not as fun to nurse sore fingers after repeated pokes with a sharp tool, though. Sometimes I totally miss when hammering a copper lid, and Bob gets to hear, "Damn it! I did it again!" as I leap away and wave a hand sporting newly crushed skin. And he *giggles*!

My type of apprenticeship with a master smith is rare. My twice-a-week visits to Bob's tin shop have allowed me to hone my skills, and the value of this workshop practicum can't be supplanted by reading any number of books.

As a female manufacturer in the tiny copper cookware-making world, I feel it is so important to save some of the oral knowledge and hands-on experience lost in the mass-manufacturing mania of the recent decades. When I show up to a tinsmith convergence—where I am sometimes the youngest person there by a decade or three (if you don't count my children)—the wealth and amount of knowledge to glean is immeasurable. The history of cookware is held within these groups, and I want to be sure it is honored and not lost.

If you find any of this information intriguing, you need to come to a tinsmith convergence. Most of the attendees are men with beards down to their midchest, and they have oodles of maker experience among them, from creating the pots and pans themselves and even the iron tools used to make them. Sit in on a class on making a pattern from scratch to reproduce a piece of old tinware, for example, and you'll hear lots of opinions on how to create cookware or lanterns or how to use certain tools or keep them working. If you have any questions at all about history, especially in the realm of kitchen and household items, these people will fill your head with so much amazing information that you'll feel you might burst. When I was just starting to conceive of my cookware line, I was given advice every time I turned around, always sincerely intended and generously offered. I've gone to convergences over the years in different spots around the country in mid-June, and I consider them must-attend events.

The first year I went, I felt super naive when Bob had me stand up in front of everyone and walk through the process of how my copper cookware was manufactured—before I'd even received the first finished piece! The guys asked me so many questions that I lost my train of thought and wasn't always able to answer. Eventually I gave up trying to sound smart.

"How heavy is the copper?" someone called out.

"Um, point zero ninety?" I answered, not sure if that was what he wanted to know.

"No, what's the weight?"

I paused. "Heavy? It's thick."

"What's the shrinkage on your handles?" the next guy asked.

"There's some," I hedged. That particular nugget of knowledge sat in my notes at home, not in Ohio with me, and certainly not memorized.

"But what percent?"

I gave up. "A tiny bit!"

Nothing like presenting metalsmithing in front of a passel of metalsmiths who are all about thirty years your senior to keep you humble. Later, some of their wives told me that the guys wouldn't have teased or asked so many questions if they didn't like me, so I felt better for feeling a bit silly!

It's rare for women to take up trades like copper- and tinsmithing. So many women have started businesses in artisan food like cheesemaking and farming and food preservation, but they haven't broken into metals in the same way. I shouldn't be one of the tiny few! We can help to carry the knowledge forward to a new generation of artisans.

COPPER AND HEAT

In centuries past, chefs and bakers knew that copper allowed for the fastest heat and the quickest cooling even if they didn't understand the exact science. Copper's heat dissipates so quickly that vintage smiths who brazed (created "bronze glue" by basically welding copper with tin at a very hot temperature) were constantly fighting the flow of the heat needed to bond a cramp seam, as any attached handles or even the air itself pulls off the heat insanely fast. I still run into this problem when working with copper in the garage and putting new tin on the cleaned interior of a pot I'm refurbishing.

People have a better understanding of how cast iron conducts heat, so when I say copper conducts fast, even heat, the conversation goes like this:

"Oh, even heat! Like cast iron?"

"No," I say. "Not really. When cast iron heats, it absorbs heat slowly and unevenly at first."

Which is true. Cast iron has hot spots. Put a thin coat of flour on the bottom of a cast-iron skillet and turn on the heat. You'll see where the flour gets darker in some places before others. Those are your hot spots.

"So cast iron *doesn't* heat evenly?"

"No," I say again, spreading my hands (I always talk with my hands, sometimes too much). "It does. But the heat is even only *after* you've spent a while warming the whole skillet and letting the hot spots mesh with the rest of the skillet. Copper, on the other hand, heats uniformly from the very start. No hot spots. Even, uniform, near-instant heat. It's why we use copper wires in our walls for electricity."

Thermal conductivity (how well and fast a metal conducts heat) plays a great part in the physics, application, and use of kitchen tools. Not only does copper have superb heat conductivity (meaning it moves energy through itself very quickly and easily), second only to silver, but the instant evenness means you can use a lower temperature than you would need to get the same results in a stainless-steel pot and thus use less energy (copper conducts heat 25 times faster than stainless steel). And copper cools very fast, too, which is why it's a perfect match for any finicky recipe and for extreme control of cooking temperatures. You know how if you don't watch certain foods, they'll start to scorch when you don't remove them from the pot right away? Not with copper. Shut off the heat and the temperature of the metal starts to drop immediately.

Going back to the question of linings, copper cookware can be lined with a material that can bond molecularly to the copper body, such as tin or silver. In other instances, the copper is mixed with other elements, such as boron and zirconium, so it can more easily be pressed next to a stainless-steel sheet. From that "bimetal," one can create stainless-steel-lined cookware. The interior lining of a copper pot can be made of any of these metals—tin and stainless steel are the most common—but you do need some metal bonded to the interior of copper cooking pots to make them food safe. Tin-lined copper cookware has been around for several hundred years, and stainless-steel-lined copper cookware has been around for many decades. It's usually personal preference in terms of lining, and I'll bring it up again later, but for now, just know that the difference between vintage lining (tin) and more modern lining (stainless steel) is rooted in heat, speed, and energy efficiency.

Once manufacturers figured out they could make a bimetal and line copper pots with stainless steel (or place a thin copper coating on a stainless-steel pot to look good and trick the public to pay higher prices), the practice of using stainless-steel rivets to attach handles became the norm. Although copper rivets may be thought of as costly, quaint, or vintage, they still have a purpose. Shake those handles before you buy!

When it comes to cookware, cheaper is rarely better. If it seems too good to be true, it probably is. Generally speaking, if it's cheap, it probably won't last long. And if it's cheap . . . well, it isn't really heirloom.

Notice the large vintage stockpot with a cover next to my small House Copper stockpot with the cover? That was the goal: modern-made cookware lined with tin to echo older cookware shapes.

INTERVIEW WITH **VALÉRIE GILBERT**, SEVENTH-GENERATION OWNER OF

MAUVIEL

Based in Villedieu-les-Poêles, France, Mauviel is one of the oldest copper cookware manufacturers still operating in Europe today. While they do create other cooking pots, they are world renowned for their copper pieces, which are made with solid, pure copper and either lined with stainless steel or hand-tinned by their extremely specialized tinners. Valérie Gilbert is focused on keeping the romance and nostalgia infused in Mauviel's copper. For many chefs, the name Mauviel is a staple, and their cookware is known for craftsmanship, longevity, and beauty.

What do you believe to be the touchstone for copper cookware's enduring legacy in the world? Why do we still make it even as technology has created new materials for cookware?
Copper represents resistance, history, tradition, and chefs' preference. We still make it because it is the best conductor of heat, precision, history, and beauty but also as it is the best material ever for cooks.

What do you believe copper brings to the modern cookware discussion?
Copper is original. It has been developed and improved to create, as far as we are concerned, new lines of copper pots inspired from the traditional ones but adapted with today's cooking habits and tastes in mind.

With the long history behind Mauviel's copper cookware creation, what has been the biggest change in the company's manufacture of copperware?
In 1995, we developed our multilayered stainless-steel-lined copper cookware, which was a big change from only tin-lined wares. Recently, copper is coming back as a fashionable material, thanks to the return of table service as a showpiece on our tables. We develop oven-to-table wares with designers now that are products for the home in a way we didn't before.

What do you like best about being a copper cookware creator?
I like the passionate challenge of revolutionizing traditions to keep those traditions alive every day. Copper is history and heritage.

As a woman, what is the biggest hurdle to overcome in the cookware industry?
I'd like to have, at the end of the day, people say I'm not a woman but just a person with passion to keep the history of our family and company, so we can be in the modern world without losing any of our heritage.

A sweet little Mauviel sugar pot, holding
1.25 quarts. Great for making chocolate!

What's a Coefficient of Thermal Expansion?

What follows is a bit of a science lesson, but knowing even a tiny bit about coefficient of thermal expansion numbers will help you understand your cookware at home and what to look for when you're buying new pieces. Coefficient numbers measure how a material expands (gets fatter, for example) when heated. The lower a coefficient number, the slower it heats. The higher the number, the faster it heats. For most cookware, you want something faster, because it takes far less energy to do the same amount of cooking. Of course this information isn't available on product packaging, so it's up to you to do your own research if you're truly interested.

Thermal conductivity is the rate/speed that heat passes through a certain material (such as copper, tin, iron, or clay—in order of speed!). The higher the number, the faster your cookware gets hot, using the least amount of energy to get it hot. (I feel like there's some sort of sex joke in there, but the science is distracting me.) Again, this information isn't something you'll see advertised on cookware packaging—but once you understand the metals used for cookware, you'll reach for cast iron for slow, long-lasting heat and copper for quick sautés and delicate sauces.

Along with a metal's retention of heat, the way in which items are assembled using particular metals, rivets, or interiors also affects how a particular piece of cookware performs and whether it will stand the test of time.

Chemistry and fire, it seems, happen in the very fibers of the cooking pot as well as in the food itself.

Molecular vs. Mechanical Bonds

Molecular Bond: In the world of metal and chemistry, a molecular bond causes the electrons of the material to exchange during the heating process, creating a new metal or alloy. This type of bonding is extremely tight. For example, when you heat up tin and copper, they will exchange electrons and an alloy (bronze) will form, a single molecule thick, between the copper on one side and the tin on the other. This kind of bond does not break. You'll wear down one metal from cooking, polishing, or cleaning, but you'll never pop this kind of bond apart.

Mechanical Bond: With mechanical bonding, metals lie next to each other but do not connect. You can treat the metals prior to heating so they lock together, a bit like Velcro, but they cannot exchange atoms. I found this out the hard way when I thought I could apply the chromium (chrome) lining to a copper pan just like I did with tin—but there was a complication. Because the metals would not bond molecularly, there was a good chance the chromium would flake off into people's food over time. Yuck! Now you know why there are no chrome-lined copper pots in my cookware!

Different pots and pans have different thicknesses.
Right: A pressed lid of thick 1.5-mm copper

COPPER THICKNESS

Thin copper sheets were common prior to the 1800s because we didn't have the machinery to work with the thicker copper. We now know that copper cookware performs best in that magical realm between 1.5 mm and 3 mm. Anything thinner will not result in cookware with "ideal" speed. Most manufacturers will tout their copper thickness if it hits 1.5 mm or above. If they don't talk about it, it's probably thinner. Marketers know what's hot, so since copper's in fashion, they'll spray or paint copper on the outside of their wares or add a thin layer of copper on the outside. Don't be afraid to ask, or at least Google a maker's background, before pulling out your credit card.

An awesome 3-mm-thick copper pot wall

CHOOSING COPPERWARE

While no one should dictate what every kitchen needs, I'm a firm believer that any avid cook worth his or her salt (pun intended) will likely want to use copper cookware at some point in their culinary lifetime. There are two distinct types of copper cookware available on the market today. Stainless-steel-lined copper cookware is easier to find and a tad less expensive. Tin-lined copper cookware is more authentically heirloom, performs faster (more science to come later), and is always handmade because there's no way a machine can make tin-lined copperware.

The Saucier

Saucier pans are made for recipes that require almost constant stirring. Usually with sloping sides and available in various heights and diameters, sauciers are traditional pans created when sauces became a cornerstone of French cuisine. Look for a size that not only fits in your kitchen (or hangs sexily from the hooks above your head) and on your stove but will hold the average sauce recipe. Typically, saucier pans are not huge by design, and you'll likely find them in sizes ranging from 4 to 8 inches in diameter. A 7-inch-wide saucier is a good place to start. Note that these pans do not have very tall sides.

The Sauté Pan

Many people are used to seeing sauté (or *sauteuse*) pans with sloping sides. In a traditional sauté pan, these sides allow foods to "jump" around while the cook stirs vigorously. Slope-sided pans are still quite useful, but if you're trying to go for a true sauté pan, look for a *sautoir*, which traditionally meant a sauté pan with a very thick bottom. Now the term is used for straight-sided sauté pans, which can be preferable because you get almost 30 percent more surface area to cook on. These come in a range of sizes from small (less than a quart) to standard 1 quart to a few quarts. I prefer the sautoir design because it not only offers a broader cooking surface but is more versatile as a kitchen tool. Sometimes this piece of cookware is also called a skillet.

The Rondeau

Though the rondeau (or *rondin*) is basically a sautoir—or straight-sided sauté pan—it is generally a sturdy piece of cookware in that it's lower but wide, as it was traditionally used for cooking bigger meals or chunky vegetables. A rondeau is typically short sided, with symmetrical short handles on either side to allow for a solid grip when full of food and heavy.

The Saucepan

Traditional saucepans (or *casseroles* in the French) come in a wide variety of sizes, from 1-quart capacities to gallons. Most pans have a single long handle on one side, and the larger pans will have a "helper" handle opposite to help with moving bigger, heavier saucepans when they're full. The sides of the saucepan are higher than those on a saucier or sauté pan, going up over a foot or more on larger pieces. The saucepan is a fantastic workhorse in the kitchen, able to handle most jobs, and is a great first piece to invest in when just getting started with a set of copperware. Fair warning: Once you start collecting, it may be hard to stop, and you'll find yourself coveting all the different sizes and diameters available.

The Stockpot

The French call a basic stockpot a *faitout*, and it is meant for all domestic uses. A really big stockpot can also be called a marmite. Taller than it is wide, the stockpot has straight sides and usually is paired with a lid. American makers who used copper sheets to make copperware called their stockpots cooking pots or boilers or kettles. Most traditional stockpots have two stout handles on either side of the pot for ease of carrying when full (they are similar to the look of a rondeau), though some early American wares had one long curved handle that swung over the top (commonly called a bail) so that you could hang the pot over a cooking fire instead of inserting it into an oven. The French call that type of handled copper pot a *porte-diner*.

The Fish Poacher (Poissonnière)

The fish poacher is a bit of a luxury, but for serious cooks it's useful for cooking the delicate flesh of all kinds of fish. Long, nearly rectangular, and made with stout handles on the short ends of the pan, the poacher always needs a cover. You'll be putting this in the oven, not on the stove, and it will give you incredible finesse when cooking seafood.

The Bowl

Copper bowls are traditionally unlined and used for whipping egg whites, as the copper reacts positively with the proteins in the whites, creating the best results for meringues, soufflés, quiches, and pretty much any other egg dishes out there. I use them for pancakes and cookie batter, too. Vintage copper bowls are typically heavy, with an iron or copper band or wire under the bead (that curled edge on the top) to keep the edge's shape. Without the band inside the bead, a copper bowl made of thin metal might see the rim crushed or split with time. Thicker copper bowls are more expensive but will not warp, dent, or smash nearly as easily. Most have a single handle made of copper or brass on one side to allow you to secure the bowl when you whisk.

The Jam Pot

For the cook who is serious about making sweets, baked goods, and jams, a copper jam pot is invaluable. These, like the bowls, are unlined, because you want the copper to interact with the sugar while heating and cooking it. A serious pastry chef wants the exact crystal changes that occur in sugar's molecules if it is directly in contact with copper while heated, resulting in sugar that doesn't clump, as well as the best control of that heat without the sugar pooling. Jam pots have a wide diameter with a flat bottom and quite tall, sloping sides. Handles do not need to be very strong; you may find some fashioned out of brass, though iron handles are found, too. The top edge is beaded and curled over, as on a copper bowl, for strength and durability.

In 2018, Giulia began running the family business of making copper cookware. When I met her, she didn't even have her new business cards yet! Her Italian family centers their life on love and food and making memories, which goes hand in hand with the philosophy of creating heirloom cookware made to last. There are many varieties within the Ruffoni brand, with different copper lining interiors, handles, and designs. Giulia is excited to be the first woman in her family to take over the well-known cookware manufacturing company, and I'm behind her all the way!

What is your favorite part about making heirloom cookware, particularly copper cookware?

In a family of Italian coppersmiths, so much of life revolved around the preparation, serving, and sharing of food. I believe that owning and understanding heirloom cookware can inspire people to gather around the stove and the table, and I love the fact that what we do can help people everywhere rediscover the love of food and the joy of conviviality.

How do you believe our understanding of the cookware in our kitchens adds to the food discussion happening around the world?

The history of human evolution is also the history of food, its ingredients, and the cooking vessels and techniques to prepare them. For thousands of years, whenever the human condition improved and people found themselves with access to more wealth and better resources, some of those resources were dedicated to improving the quality and variety of the foods we consumed. During the European Renaissance in particular, the court's smiths and cooks would work closely together, with the former constantly inventing and improving on vessels and tools to enable the latter to devise new recipes and cooking techniques. It was a virtuous circle of innovation, which continued into the nineteenth century and led to massive improvements in both the taste and nutritional value of what people ate.

Then came the era of mass production and economies of scale; agricultural advancements started focusing on quantity at the expense of quality, and as people became busier and food cheaper, the preparation of meals got increasingly outsourced, from the home kitchen to restaurants, fast-food chains, and large-scale factories. Similarly, cookware started being produced at larger scale and lower cost but often also at lower quality. Thankfully, this trend is now being reversed, with a growing appreciation for real food that is seasonal, local, and, increasingly, homemade. As real food demands real cooking, we will rediscover the value of owning a few quality pieces of cookware that deliver what they promise and can stand the test of time. I still own and treasure my grandmother's copper pots, which have made many, many delicious risottos and, with some polish, are still as good as new.

As a woman in the family business (are you the first?), what challenges does that bring, if any?

I am the first woman in the family business who was born with the Ruffoni last name, but I am following in the footsteps of other women who have played a critical role in the business. My mother and grandmother have both been instrumental to the birth and growth of Ruffoni: They probably don't get mentioned enough in the telling of our family history, but as they say, "Behind every great man . . ." My father is recognized as a coppersmith, appreciated for his ability to conjugate the art and traditions of cookware shapes with technical ability and know-how, but he is the first to acknowledge that a key success factor for our cookware is understanding how it will be used, and what features are needed for different dishes. This deep understanding of food preparation and a genuine empathy with our customers— home chefs who have traditionally been mostly women—always came from the women in the family! So as a woman in the business, the biggest challenge ahead of me is also my biggest opportunity: to be able to incorporate the traditional expertise of how food is cooked with the technical understanding of how to make cookware—all while being taken seriously as the youngest kid on the block!

If you could make any piece of copper cookware with your own hands, what would it be and why?

I especially love the various vessels that are designed for a specific purpose so that one can really appreciate the value of having cooked with copper in the final dish—the zabaglione bowl, the risotto pan, the polenta pot—but what I most wish I could do with my own hands is the hand-tinning process. The way in which our master tinners use the purest tin and very hot flames and then hand-brush each individual piece is mesmerizing to watch. To be fair, the use of copper-coated stainless steel is certainly more practical, and I often cook in it myself, but the superior heat conductivity and history of tin-lined copper cookware remain unparalleled.

Did You Know?

You've heard the saying "You've got too many irons in the fire," especially if you're one of those people (I'm guilty of it!) who likes to do a lot of things at once. Sometimes it's completely manageable, and other times not. The original meaning of the expression comes from coppersmiths and tinsmiths. Once they stopped making mostly cookware, smiths started to do a lot of roofs made of tin and copper sheet and gutter work on houses. To seal up the work, they'd have to solder (use tin as "metal glue") any seams. Small braziers, or portable furnaces, were hung on the roofs next to the smiths, and they'd insert handheld soldering irons inside the furnace opening where coals were heaped. As they used one "copper"—or soldering iron—the other one or two would be heating, so they could be used immediately as needed. It was a rhythmic juggle. Use one iron, heat two, switch as the one you're holding cools.

Copper conducts heat and loses heat so fast that smiths who braze were constantly fighting the flow of the heat needed to bond a seam, so they needed to move fast. But put too many soldering copper irons in the little brazier at once? None of them would get hot enough to do a proper job. The notion translates to our daily lives with much the same meaning!

INTERVIEW WITH DAN MOORE,
MASTER TINNER AND TINNING SPECIALIST

Dan is the tinner in Ohio who taught me how to line copper pots with tin using centuries-old method of hand-wiping molten metal along the interior of the copperware. The first time he showed me (and everyone at the tinsmith convergence), he started a propane fire at a historic village. He covered vintage pieces with lime paste, and wiped these perfect interiors while explaining what he was doing. It looked so casual and easy! Dan said he expected me to try it. I put on long pants and one of the guys covered my exposed feet with a rag (once again I didn't have steel-toe boots), and I tinned one of my own copper lids. And you know what? It turned out amazing!

How can you prepare copperware to get retinned or repaired?
Box it up safely and add a letter explaining what you want done to the copper. For instance, if you want dents out, make a note of it. Some tinners won't remove those dents unless told to do so. That's not out of laziness but out of respect for the copper's history. Handles are tightened by the tinner, or rivets are replaced, if needed, for a few extra dollars.

How can you tell if your copper has been tinned properly?
Look for smoothness and uniform tin over the whole inside. There shouldn't be any clumping or black spots. If you see black, under it is copper, not tin. Tin should not be on the outside of the pot when you receive your piece back unless it is done by a European tinner or a tinner replicating European methods. Tinners trained in Europe are known to put about a half inch of tin around the outside top lip of copperware. Always research when looking for a retinner; there are too many fake fly-by-night types. .

What do you like best about being a tinner?
History was my favorite subject in school. Retinning a piece that came from the Ritz or some other famous places that had their name stamped on the side and that had once catered to all the elites of the past makes you wonder. Did Marilyn Monroe eat a dish that was made in this copper pot? Was she with JFK when she did? I've done pieces with the royal family stamp on them, old pieces from the Royal Navy of years past. The stories that pop in my head are endless. But the real reward is seeing the excitement from ones who have a piece that belonged to a mom, dad, or grandma that has been in the family for years.

If you follow the stock market on TV for metals and raw materials, you'll see the cost of gold, silver, and copper listed along the bottom of the screen. Take notice of how copper is always on the high side in terms of metal cost. Pure, true copper needs to be pulled from the earth, cleaned, refined, smelted, rolled, and prepared. My copper needs to be deoxidized with phosphorous (so the tin lining sticks better) for use. That's not cheap, and copper itself is still incredibly valuable as a raw material. An average-size pure copper pot may contain several pounds of solid copper. For instance, the 12-inch copper skillet I make weighs 7 1/2 pounds. Remove the handle, which is about 1 pound, and there's still 6 1/2 pounds of copper in that pan. If the piece is made by a real copper manufacturer (not shipped in from a knockoff factory), there will also be some handwork that went into its creation. This can range from spinning the copper sheet or attaching the rivets (as I do) to, in the case of tin linings, hand-wiping the tin plus giving the copper a final cleaning (me again).

So you're paying for the material and hands-on craftsmanship—a combination of old and new skills—which creates a piece of cookware (artwork, really) that could last thousands of years. Remember, we still find copper cookware used by the ancient Egyptians.

Let's admit that the desire to purchase fancy-looking, inexpensive cookware, which always seems to be on sale, is beyond tempting! Say you spent twenty dollars on that pan from your local big-box store. Within three years (probably less), the nonstick plastic and paint is chipping and it no longer works like a charm with eggs, so you toss it and buy another pan—the next model that happens to be on sale. If you live to be eighty, you might purchase twenty pans in your lifetime, costing you four hundred dollars with nothing to show for it afterward, except your contribution to a nearby landfill. And that's just one pot. Presumably you want several pots and skillets in your kitchen, so now you could end up spending thousands of dollars on inferior cookware.

Instead, what if you spend four hundred dollars on a copper piece that will last so long you can bequeath it to your children? And they can do the same for their children. And nothing ends up in a landfill! Copper doesn't usually need to get tossed; when it needs a little love, you just send it off for

Towering pines reflected in the
bottom of a super-shiny copper pan

refurbishment and keep using it for generations. I mean, what's not to love?

Over the years, I've received many pots, pans, kettles, and cups that have had intense wear and tear, or simply a lot of caring use, to be repaired or relined with tin. Much of my work involves refurbishing instead of building cookware from scratch, and I've worked on some truly amazing pieces and some extremely difficult items! For instance, one small covered pot, built in the reproduction-ware style Bob typically makes, had been left next to a fire. That's typically not a problem, but in this case someone had put a lighter in the pot and forgotten about it. When the pot got too hot, that lighter went off with a *bang!* and flew across the campsite, or so the owner told me. You better believe the lid was misshapen, the bottom bellied out, the sides dented, and the tin completely destroyed. Another pot I had to re-

The tinner's bench in my garage, with tools and both older and new cookware in various states of fixin'

store was gigantic—so big that I couldn't hold it up to any tools for cleaning or fit it in any acid-soaking bath for stripping out the forty years of cooking grime and old oxidized tin. I ended up holding a buffing wheel with a metal stripping attachment vertically over the pot and slowly removing the old dirt. That was definitely an inappropriate use of a tool, but I didn't know how else to manage it!

Sometimes I'll get copper pans and skillets made in a country where the copper itself isn't very good quality or very thick. Those pieces don't always take the tin well, even if I try to retin them five times in a row. It gets so frustrating, and I've actually thought myself incompetent—until I realized it wasn't me, it was the copper! Add some aluminum rivets, which reject tinning altogether, and you can have a perfect storm of mishaps.

Working on old teapots is tricky because it's hard for me to squeeze my hand inside to do the cleaning and the tinning, and if the pot gets too hot when I'm tinning it, the spout can fall off! One time I was working on copper cups that were put together so poorly that they fell completely apart, in four pieces, over the fire. They went back together, of course, but the first time that happened, I was definitely shocked and nervous about handling them!

The bottom line? No matter how old or bruised or damaged those pieces were, they all were fixable and usable once again! Not too bad for the "cost" of copper!

BUYING COPPER COOKWARE

Copper has become less a tool of ancient battles, or our stoves, and more a piece of the stock market race as time has marched on. Do you recall the Daddy Warbucks line that he shouted into his phone in the play *Annie*: "Buy copper! More copper!" (Or is that just me loving one of the older versions?) Copper cookware fell out of fashion, out of style, and out of the everyday kitchen about one hundred years ago. Part of the blame for this fact falls on the less expensive cast-iron cookware, which was being manufactured by the end of the 1700s. But it might be more than that. We're just kind of lazy sometimes, and copper requires a little extra care to stay pretty (though letting it get a rich patina doesn't hurt it one bit). Remember the show *Downton Abbey*? There's a team of cooks and kitchen staff who handled everything from breakfast to tea to dinner, and the use of copper was properly portrayed in the large kitchens well through the first decades of the 1900s. I know I don't have a slew of housekeepers and cooks to keep my cookware polished. If it hadn't been for learning the science behind my cookware, I likely would have never owned copper cookware (and my mother never would have either)!

The Hunt for Vintage Copper

Hitting up a flea market for some vintage copper? If you don't have a copy of *Les cuivres de cuisine* by Jean-Claude Renard or *American Copper & Brass* by Henry J. Kauffman on hand, you'll have to learn what to look for and how to know if what you're fondling is antique cookware or just something that hasn't been polished in twenty years.

Vintage copper will be tin lined. It may have a very black interior (meaning the tin is super old or very dirty and could use a nice cleaning or retinning), or the tin may be completely worn away and you'll see patches of the copper itself coming through on the interior. Sometimes a pot's interior is lined with nickel, so if you have a nickel allergy, send it to a tinner for checking, cleaning, and retinning. (Note: Tinners no longer use nickel on copper interiors because of the allergy potential. A nickel-lined piece will get stripped and new food-grade pure tin applied to the interior instead.)

Vintage copper may also have a maker's mark on the bottom or along the side, usually near the handle. If you can locate such a mark, you're in luck and can research the history of the creator of your piece.

If, however, you are wandering flea market stalls or a local thrift store and see a bunch of dusty copper on the shelves and the interior looks relatively new, it's probably only a few decades old. Copper cookware was always lined with tin until almost 1940. Revere Ware, in the service of finding something more "durable" than tin, created its first stainless-steel copper-clad line in 1936. You'll see the telltale signs of a stainless interior by noting how the silver-colored interior has faint spinning marks, looking much like the patterned rings of a chopped-down tree. Don't pay too much for these pots unless you like the old patina look. You're essentially buying a stainless-steel pot with copper plate on the outside. Hold out for the truly remarkable finds; people might charge forty dollars for a piece if they don't know the true value. Vintage pieces can sell into the hundreds of dollars.

The cookware pieces in the middle and left, including the lid, are 100 percent handmade reproductions of vintage designs (the one on the left is a type of boiler and mug combo called a "mucket" while the middle one is a kettle from the fur trade era). The pot on the far right is a rare vintage piece, with handmade cramp seams shown along the bottom.

Choosing Modern Copper Cookware

As I mentioned earlier, copper cookware performs best in that magical realm between 1.5 mm and 3 mm, and that's what modern makers try to hit. Typically, but not always, stainless-steel-lined copper pots on the market today consist primarily of stainless steel with a thin copper exterior, so the cookware *performs* like a stainless-steel pot. (Again, if the pot seems like a good price, it's probably because you're just paying for a stainless pot that's been "prettied up" with a bit of copper for looks, not actual performance.)

While we're discussing construction, I want to offer up another tidbit to help you find true, solid, heirloom copper cookware. Check out the handles. Traditional copperware has copper or brass handles sometimes fitted with a wooden dowel to allow for easier handling when hot—watch the introductory credits of *Downton Abbey* and you'll see what I mean. Here is the key: The handles are attached to the body with only copper rivets.

Back in the day, after coppersmiths crafted a boiler or a pot out of a sheet of copper, they secured a handle—long, flat, or in a conical design—with copper rivets that heated and cooled at the same speed as the body of the pot. This ensured a tight seal and fit of the handle to the curve of the pot. Without copper rivets, a perfect seal was not always possible, which caused the handle to become loose and rattle. Even more upsetting is that the weight of the handle pulled at the softer copper and ultimately distorted or bowed the copper body. Modern-day smiths know to use copper rivets, and now so do you!

So now you're asking, *Then why are many commercial manufacturers using stainless-steel rivets instead of copper? Sara, didn't you just say that copper rivets are required to create a sound pan with handles and interior linings that work together well?*

There are a few reasons for this shortcut. One is cost. Stainless steel is less expensive. Second, copper rivets will not bond to a stainless interior; they kind of "sit together" with extreme variations in how quickly they'll react to heat. It's worth noting that ferrous metals (containing iron), such as stainless steel, and nonferrous (without iron), such as copper, do not bond on a molecular level (see "Molecular vs. Mechanical Bonds" on page 71). The exception: Ferrous and nonferrous metals can bond a bit if copper has been mixed with other metals to form a copper alloy that will allow for slower conductivity/cooking, but the alloyed copper will create a closer relationship to the coefficients of thermal expansion between stainless steel and copper. This means that if you combine copper with materials such as boron, which has a slower coefficient of thermal expansion, you can "slow down" the copper, making it sit more nicely next to stainless steel, which is also slower. Make sense?

The Endless Lining Debate

There are pros and cons for the two main types of lined copper cookware—tin and stainless steel—and people tend to align themselves with one of these camps. Whatever you choose, always look to see if the manufacturer explains the metals used; unfortunately, the cheaper the item is, the likelier it's been poorly constructed. Serious copper cookware is not meant to be bought from mass retailers who offer items that could probably be found on Alibaba or in a big-box chain store for less than fifty dollars. If you're really going to cook with copper and build yourself an heirloom kitchen, find pure metal copper cookware made of nothing but copper and tin or copper and stainless steel. If the manufacturer or maker discusses the thickness of the copper, you're in luck! You've found a solid company selling authentic wares.

Copper rivets, handles, and a Mauviel pot. You can't go wrong with lots of copper!

	TIN-LINED COPPER COOKWARE	STAINLESS-STEEL-LINED COPPER COOKWARE
PROS	Copper thickness is 1.5 mm to 3 mm.	Copper thickness is 1.5 mm to 3 mm.
	Cookware is made from pure copper and tin metals (no alloys), so no surprise metals getting into your food!	Cookware is food safe.
		Metal whisks and other tough utensils can be used on the interior.
	Cookware is food safe.	The interior does not need any upkeep.
	Tin lining is naturally nonstick.	
	Tin is a micronutrient our bodies need.	The hard interior has a high melting point.
	Tin is molecularly bonded to copper (no chipping).	Copper exterior will not rust.
	Pure tin will not rust.	
	Copper exterior will not rust.	
CONS	Low melting point: If you heat an empty tin-lined pot past 420°F, the tin will start to soften.	Stainless steel is mechanically bonded to copper, so over time it will pop apart from the copper body.
	Cookware needs retinning after 15 years of daily use.	Stainless steel is 25 times less conductive than copper, so it heats slowly.
	No metal utensils should be used.	Cookware interior can pit or react to salt.
	Cookware is generally not dishwasher safe.	Cookware is generally not dishwasher safe.
	Cookware cannot be used on induction stovetops.	Cookware cannot be used on induction stovetops.
	Tin can darken over time, making the interior look "dirty" if not properly cleaned.	Sticky food will stick to stainless and require a lot of scrubbing.
		Cookware can darken over time, making the interior look "dirty" if not properly seasoned.
		Cookware contains iron and will eventually rust.

ROCKY MOUNTAIN RETINNING

This 50-pound stockpot "pushed me to my physical limit," Erik recalls.

Thanks to social media, our tiny group of restorers can connect. I met Erik through Instagram, and we spent time hanging out in Denver after a tour of his workspace, drinking old-fashioneds and talking shop. Erik was trained by his father and is passionate about linings for copper pans, the science behind them, and what makes a tradesperson an artisan.

What kinds of difficulties might you find while doing a restoration job?

Cleaning the interior surfaces of most copper vessels. Days of soaking in acids and bases with abrasively hand-scrubbing the interiors until they are clean enough for good adhesion of tin. Also, dent removal can be tedious and time consuming.

What do you like best about refurbishing copper?

I enjoy restoring everything, to be honest. Giving new life to a piece is unexplainable. I had an elderly couple come to the shop. They had bought a copper frying pan some sixty years ago, and it had extreme sentimental value. When they picked it up after I had restored it, they both were in tears because of how beautiful it looked again. They were so grateful and happy. These moments when you touch someone's heart make what we do priceless!

What do you believe are the hallmarks of a good hand-tinning job?

Good tinning consists of a smooth mirror finish. Of course, wipe marks are present but smooth. Also, tinning over nickel linings will prevent you from having a mirror shine. Scratches should be cleaned out, so they do not turn black during tinning. In fact, it's unacceptable to have any spots where the tin doesn't take. I see this very often and I find this occurrence is accepted by the masses, but people need to be educated that this does not qualify as a high-quality tinning standard.

What do you believe is a reason tin-lined copper has generally fallen out of favor in kitchens?

I believe it's due to the lack of exposure and education. Manufacturers have done a very poor job of educating their consumers on how to care for and use it.

An Abbreviated History of Stainless-Steel-Lined Copper Cookware

Although I obviously prefer and work with tin-lined copper pans, everyone gets some love in this book! Stainless-steel interiors vary depending on the manufacturer. The thickness of the stainless steel, the elemental makeup of it, and the quality of the metal itself are different among makers and countries of origin. American manufacturers of copper cookware went slowly out of business, and by the end of the 1970s, Waldo in New York was the only one still creating copper. One of my go-to references, Henry Kauffman's 1995 book *American Copper & Brass*, discusses different copper pieces up to the 1860s in terms of identifying the maker's marks on tin-lined copper cookware, and unfortunately the production of such wares has declined tremendously since then. Those who continued to produce copperware in France, Italy, and Belgium, and later in India and China, use stainless steel in almost all their pots and pans. They continue to do so today with remarkable success.

Part of this switch to stainless-steel cookware stemmed from a demand in the postwar West for "easier" and less expensive cookware. People wanted cookware with an interior that required less care. The notion that cookware could (and should) become disposable seeped into the culture with the postwar aluminum cookware sets as well. Performance, tradition, and even craftsmanship were sacrificed more and more. This means, as I have mentioned, that you may find a pot that seems to be copper on the outside, but it's actually a stainless-steel or aluminum pot dressed up to look like copper. These pots aren't necessarily bad, but you shouldn't spend much money on them. Is *knockoff* too strong a word here?

Most cooks (and probably even noncooks) know that stainless steel is hardy and sturdy. You can be very tough on it, and though food sticks to it easily and you have to scrub hard to clean it, some people put their stainless-steel-lined copper in the dishwasher because they trust the solidness of steel. I wouldn't recommend ever putting copper, no matter the lining, in the dishwasher, but that's just my opinion. I like to keep my copper pretty and not pitted.

My science lesson now turns to an observation about metal activity. Stainless steel doesn't conduct heat as quickly as pure copper, nor do stainless steel and copper heat and cool at the same rate. The two metals sit together most of the time, but they slowly bend away from each other until they can (and sometimes do) warp and pop apart. Stainless-steel-lined cookware is relatively young compared with tin-lined copper, and I tend to skew toward cookware that's tried and true. Still, I'd put some stainless-steel-lined copper cookware into the heirloom category simply because it has been around for decades and looks like it's here to stay. Plus, there are heirloom companies that have discovered how to design a copper and stainless-steel pot that is extremely high quality and will last generations.

Some stainless-steel-lined copper is not simply just stainless steel with thin copper on the exterior, but a true bimetal. Falk, out of Belgium, has created a patented combination that is a copper alloy containing a mix of zirconium, titanium, aluminum, and boron with a chromium and nickel-mixed stainless steel pressed together into an authentic bimetal. If you want to go the stainless-steel route for your copper cookware, look for this type of product. I can't fault any company trying to put copper back into all kitchens. Just do your research. Pick a company that will tell you up front what their pots are made from and the thickness of their copper (you want it to be at least 1.5 mm thick).

Why Not Use Aluminum Lining on Copper Cookware?

This question has been asked of me in the past, and it's one I struggled with when I first started making cookware. Here's what I discovered:

Aluminum, like tin, actually does bond to copper if it is heated beyond 1022°F. The exchange of electrons creates a thick molecule of copper aluminide, which is more than just an alloy of copper and aluminum, but for cookware's sake, the two metals bond somewhat like tin and copper. So at first I thought aluminum could be a great candidate for lining copper cookware. But there was more to it.

I found that although aluminum marries extremely fast with oxygen and copper, it creates a film, or oxide, that interferes with any attempt at combining the two metals. In fact, many metallurgists feel the only way to create a bond is friction welding, but the result would not be conducive to making cookware. In the end, it would take an incredible amount of energy, time, and money to create something that costs more to make than tin-lined copper but does not conduct heat any better. (Oh, and I have no idea how to do it other than in an oxygen-void vacuum.)

Cooking up some fish and mushrooms with lemon in tin-lined copper over an outdoor open campfire

COOKING WITH COPPER COOKWARE

Cooking with tin-lined copper and cooking with stainless-steel-lined copper differ because of the interior metals and how they react to heat. Copper heats and cools very fast, of course, but the lining will really determine the way your food cooks.

THE RULES FOR TIN-LINED COPPER

- Always have food or liquid in the pan before heating it.
- Never use sharp or metal utensils—you'll scratch the tin.
- Remember to use appropriate hand protection when cooking—the metal holds heat long after you remove it from the source.

THE RULES FOR STAINLESS-STEEL-LINED COPPER

- Food can be added before or after heating begins.
- Remember to use appropriate hand protection when cooking—the metal holds heat long after you remove it from the source.

You already know I'm totally and completely biased about copper. I think it's the hottest, most beautiful, and longest-lasting metal to cook with—but that love doesn't help get it clean!

I know people have trepidations about caring for copper cookware. I made my mother some pots, but she didn't use them for more than a year because she was nervous about wrecking them during cooking and especially cleaning! I said, "Mom, you have cast-iron skillets. Copper is no more difficult. In some ways, it's easier because you don't have to keep rust off." She took a deep breath, cooked in a copper pan . . . and promptly fell in love.

We've discussed the two kinds of copper cookware: tin lined and stainless steel lined. Tin-lined copper cookware, with its ability to be relined, can last centuries, which is why I like to call it renewable. Stainless-steel-lined copper cookware has yet to see its one hundredth birthday, so I really cannot speak to its longevity, but for now we should assume it will last a few generations at the very least.

So, let's dive in! To start, here are some general tips.

Cleaning food burned onto the linings of copper cookware is a relatively stress-free process. Simply fill the cookware with water and boil it. The cooked-on food should come off with a soft cloth.

As with cast iron, leaving water to soak inside the cookware for days is not ideal, mainly because it can, depending on the quality of the water, cause discoloration or eat away at any lining. Food is best removed after cooking or serving, and a copper pot should be hand washed within twenty-four hours using warm water and nonabrasive soap. Dry immediately and you're set to go!

Caring for Stainless-Steel Copper Cookware Linings

Stainless-steel-lined copper pots let you be rough on the interior when cleaning. Because stainless steel tends to be a sticky metal, you'll certainly need some elbow grease to root out cooked-on food particles left behind, but this metal can handle it. You may treat the interior lining of a stainless-steel-lined copper pot the same as you'd treat a regular stainless-steel pot when cleaning. Keep it simple.

You can allow stainless-steel-lined cookware to darken. As a ferrous metal, stainless steel can essentially be seasoned as if it were cast iron.

If you do season your stainless-steel interior, it will eventually become slightly nonstick. However, many people prefer to have the bright, silvery stainless-steel-lining look and will scrub off the food particles to keep it shiny and enhance the chromium embedded in the stainless-steel makeup. This practice could eventually cause pitting and possible rusting, so use a very mild dish soap to clean the cookware and then dry thoroughly. Most manufacturers will tell you not to put the pots and pans in the dishwasher to help with the pan's life.

Caring for Tin Copper Cookware Linings

Tin-lined copper cookware is naturally nonstick and will not need much scrubbing to get clean. If treated properly, the tin will keep its nonstick properties (it's nature's Teflon!) as long as you do not use metal instruments or abrasive metal scrubbies such as SOS pads when cleaning. As with pure copper that's lined with stainless steel, you'll also want to keep tin-lined cookware out of the dishwasher. There aren't any safe dishwasher soaps on the market for tin, and tin linings last longest and best when hand washed.

Generally, tin linings can handle around fifteen years of *daily* use before they may need retinning. Though the lining does not flake or chip off owing to the molecular bond, it will thin out. A tinsmith or coppersmith can usually retin the piece after cleaning and preparing both the old tin surface and the copper exterior. Depending on the smith, a person might request the use of either a chemical or a natural (pine resin or rosin) flux, which is required to prepare the copper to chemically bond tin to the interior, though the natural flux does not provide as smooth a finish to the tin layer. A retinned pot will usually return to its owner with a new solid layer of hand-wiped tin and a cleaned copper exterior unless the tinner is asked not to clean off the exterior patina with a polish.

If you wish to simply clean your tin after a particularly robust cooking spree, or if you've raised the heat so high that some particles of food are adhering a bit more stubbornly than usual, heating the pot filled with water and a bit of nonabrasive dish soap until the water simmers will soften the food, making it easier to remove.

Caring for All Copper Pan Exteriors

Because true copper is soft, pure copper cookware can dent with use, especially on a gas stove with cast-iron grates or with rough use in and out of the oven. This does not affect the performance of the cookware and can add to its charm and romance. Still, serious dents and gouges can sometimes be carefully raised or planished out by a professional coppersmith—so don't cry if you drop your pot.

Copper does age with time and use, and the warm exterior will eventually take on a darker patina, especially if the cookware is used over a gas or open flame cooking surface. In the beginning, such smears, fingerprints, and early dark ghosting can be removed with ketchup (favorite trick ever!). Rub the red stuff all over the copper part of the pot, let it sit for about five minutes, and then wash and dry, and that beautiful rosy glow will return to the pot. It's really the closest thing to magic I've ever seen.

To remove a little tougher discoloration on copper, use roughly two parts ketchup and one part fine sea salt devoid of silicon (check the label of your salt; a pure powder-fine pink Himalayan is a great option), and follow the steps listed above. If there are even darker marks, try the simple home concoction below. The beauty of these copper-cleaning recipes is they are natural and can be used on both tin and stainless-steel interiors, as well as the copper exterior, without worrying about damage to the lining.

Natural Copper Cleaning Recipes

Here's a natural remedy to clean copper cookware that you can use when rhubarb is in season. This mixture can both brighten tin linings and polish the exterior of copper cookware. Depending on the patina and age of the copperware, the rhubarb's activated oxalic acid can make a noticeable difference or just take the edge off the patina. Still, it's a great, nonchemical option for brightening. Bob discovered this while participating in a reenactment camp, and I've tried it since as a test. It does well for being all natural!

2 cups chopped rhubarb stalks
½ cup sugar

To clean the tin interior, place all the ingredients in the tin-lined copper pot, add enough water to cover the rhubarb, and turn the heat to medium. Cook, adding more water as needed to keep the rhubarb covered, until the rhubarb is soft and mushy, about 10 minutes. Turn off the heat and let the mixture sit in the tin for 10 minutes, then remove the mixture, gently

wash, and remove any remaining rhubarb from the tin interior. The tin will brighten wherever the rhubarb touched. Enjoy your brightened tin!

To use the rhubarb mixture to clean the copper part of the pan, simply allow the rhubarb to cool enough to handle, then spread it, paste-like, over the copper. You'll want the mixture to feel quite sticky and pasty. Let it partially dry (this will depend on the amount of humidity in the air), then wash it off with gentle soap and warm water and dry the cookware.

You can also prepare this mixture in the microwave. Place the rhubarb in a microwave-safe bowl and cook on high for up to 3 minutes, or until the rhubarb is quite soft and starting to bubble. Add the sugar and mix until a paste forms. Spoon it onto the copper or tin and let it partially cool or dry before rinsing it off.

Quick Copper Cleaning Guide for Tin- or Stainless-Steel-Lined Copper Cookware

⇒DO⇐

1. Clean within 24 hours of use.

2. Hand-wash for best results and longevity.

3. Clean using all-natural or chemical cleaners (listed below).

4. Retin old/used tin-lined copper cookware when a large amount of copper shows through the worn tin. (In the unlikely event that a stainless-steel pan wears through or if the stainless steel separates from the copper, bubbles apart, or delaminates, throw it away; it's not fixable.)

⇒DON'T⇐

1. Leave water to soak in copper cookware. Depending on the chemical makeup of your water, it can discolor or eat away the lining.

2. Use copper chemical cleaners on the linings. You can use stainless-steel cleaners on stainless-steel-lined cookware if desired, but follow the instructions to be sure the lining is cleaned and then food safe again.

3. Clean in the dishwasher.

Copper Cookware Polish

My dear friends at Brooklyn Copper Cookware created the following recipe for a deeper home polish. Combine the following in a bowl:

3 parts all-purpose flour
2 parts ketchup
2 parts fine sea salt
1 part white vinegar

Coat the paste-like substance over the entire copper exterior and let it stand for 10 minutes. This will allow the acids and chemical reactions activated by the vinegar and ketchup time to eat at the patina. After 10 minutes, rub the paste again, rinse in warm water, and wipe your copper dry.

Chemical Copper Cookware Cleaners

I would be remiss if I didn't mention some of the more commercial methods available for cleaning and polishing the exteriors of copper pots and pans (remember to avoid using chemical copper cleaners on the linings). To really scrub that copper to a shine, or to liven up vintage pieces, you may end up resorting to some nonnatural remedies for your metal. Please take care to read all the directions that come with both your cookware and the cleaners and pastes to make the care of your cookware exact and successful. There, that ought to do it.

Chemical Products

To maintain or polish copper exteriors with chemical products, there are several brands that do a lovely job. I always start with the liquid cleaner Tarn-X, quickly followed by a more protective paste polish, such as any of the products below:

MAAS polish
Bar Keepers Friend cleanser and polish
Eve Stone Antiques brass and copper polish
Wright's copper cream
Red Bear copper and brass polish
Twinkle brass and copper cleaning kit
Brasso metal polish
Flitz metal, plastic, and fiberglass polish

I've had some excellent experiences with these tools when cleaning my copperware:

1. euroSCRUBBY (perfect for cleaning tin linings)

2. Nylon net pot and pan scrubbers (for allover cleaning)

COPPER FOREVER!

Copper cookware can be viewed as a phenomenon connecting people to ancient generations and cultures. It exists perfectly between absolute elegance and campfire ruggedness, it performs ridiculously well over heat and flame, and it can be brought back to its original glory by the hands of skilled craftspeople. Pure copperware is a treasure steeped in intrinsic value that is meant to be celebrated, savored, protected, and passed on to future generations. Some retinning clients send me their pieces and say, "I picked this up at an estate sale and really love cooking in it. I don't know why, but I do!"

I do, too. To this day, after years of creating, building, cooking, cleaning, repairing, buying, or selling, I am completely infatuated with this wondrous metal for the ages. Copper's an heirloom in the truest, purest sense.

My big copper skillet right off the buffing wheel. I love how sparkly newly built copper looks!

IRON

As I mentioned earlier, my first foray into a cast-iron foundry was a bit of a disaster when I showed up in ballet flats. But the flats made it out unscathed, and so did I. Since then, I've definitely burned clothes, eyelashes, and hands over seasoning fires, but as anyone who uses cast iron knows, the fire is part of the deal. The history of cast iron is well documented but fun to visit, and it includes trivia and science, too. You'll hopefully enjoy cast iron that much more after this!

When I decided to make cast-iron skillets, the pressure was on. This kind of cookware has experienced a gigantic surge in use and popularity, and everybody has an opinion, from the history of iron to the proper seasoning oils and process. If I did it "wrong," there'd be hell to pay. Whatever pan coating I chose, someone was going to disagree with it—and there are many other points of contention. What's better, vintage or new? Seasoned with olive oil or lard? Does the smoothness make a difference or not? I knew I was jumping into a piece of the cookware puzzle that would pit my skillets against those with hundreds of years of operation behind them. There are many time-honored brands of cast-iron makers in America, and boutique shops as well, so once again, who was I—an unseasoned (pun intended) metalsmith who had never seasoned a cast-iron skillet?

To be completely honest, when I started this endeavor, I had one cast-iron skillet in my kitchen, and I was scared to use it. I didn't understand how it worked; I had a vague idea it was supposed to be good to cook in but no idea why. I'd received it as a wedding gift, and I'm frankly surprised it didn't rust completely, considering that I pulled it out with sincere trepidation about three times a year. Research, and talking to a lot of people who collected cast iron, eventually helped me overcome that worry. Also, those visits to the foundry made it all less mystical!

In a way, adding cast iron to the cookware line was harder because it was such an entrenched part of the kitchen. Unlike copper, which is not as well understood these days, cast iron had never left our stoves and ovens. But my original idea—to create a kitchenware line filled with locally made items that would have existed in a pioneer kitchen—simply *had* to include cast iron. Cast iron is a staple in our history! Plus, it was a challenge, and by now you might have noticed that I like a good learning curve! I knew that to do this right, I'd have to check in with Uncle Doug again.

I also invited friends who were die-hard cast-iron collectors over to the house, bribing them with fancy meals as long as they brought some of their wares and spilled their hearts about what they loved about vintage pieces, what to look for when collecting, and how to take care of the iron. I joined cast-iron associations, where collectors gathered and discussed and traded. I pored over old advertisements, magazines, and books about casting metals that were both inspiring and a little over my head when it came to technical information (I hoped some of it stuck via osmosis). I spoke to other makers and looked at photographs of vintage wares. What made today's cast iron different from what was made in the 1800s? How is the history of cast iron different from that of copper?

The first difference I noticed is that original cast iron had a little smoke ring on the bottom, which is not often seen in modern cast iron. Why? Because the pieces were made to fit precisely inside a hob (the circle of iron that lifts out of the top of an old potbelly stove), so you'd lift out the size circle that matched your cast-iron cookware and sit the pot right inside. The smoke ring acted as a catch and barrier to help with the fit and keep the smoke and heat inside the stove where it belongs. Amazing! So I figured that pioneers' cast-iron pans would have the rings and added one to my cast-iron designs for nostalgia's sake, not because I believe we'll be reverting back to potbelly stoves anytime soon.

I also knew cast iron used to be hung on nails (and later on racks) to dry, so I put a hole in the handle, and I put a little helper handle on the opposite side of the pan to help with weight distribution, because let's face it, we're not all hauling huge baskets of wet laundry every week anymore or doing other kinds of physically intense labor, and both John and I were well aware of the strength needed to hoist those big cast-iron pieces. My goal was to design something that was practical for today's kitchens but still nodded to the past, so I chose the classic pioneer skillet as my first experience in cast-iron design. This would be just like the standard pieces most families would have had, in various sizes, with a few historical details since lost to modernity.

I went back to the old collectors' books and rummage sales and looked at the cast iron that collectors drooled over. What would make it a classic pioneer skillet? There'd be that smoke ring for the old potbelly stoves, and a simple handle, and a basic size. I knew I'd end up hand-sanding each one, and that would add a special finish that a machine-made skillet wouldn't have; the smoothness would be a nod to the traditional skillets made with the finer sand. But it was a constant, evolutionary process to make decisions about the final look.

When Uncle Doug next came to Wisconsin, I had him look at the designs, which had been prototyped using a 3-D printer, and give his opinion on the metal thickness and detailing. There were always tweaks. Make the lip thinner . . . but not too thin. Make the logo in the bottom deeper . . . but not too deep. When they say the most difficult part about making anything is the research and development, it's totally true.

This little vintage pot comes with legs and "ears" on each side, from which a wrought-iron bail is strung so it can hang over an open fire. The piece was made using a three-part mold, and the downturn of the ears places this pot's creation likely between 1720 and 1760.

Eventually it was time to bite the bullet and make the skillets. Someone was always going to have a tweak, an idea, or a preference. I just needed to jump in and start the process in earnest.

So I called on Julia of Design Between, my product developer for the copper line, to make the last adjustments. Julia and I are both blond and blue eyed, and we each have three blond and blue-eyed kids all about the same age (when we go to reenactments together, people think we've brought a day care). Sometimes our design meetings took place in our kitchens with the kids running around in *Frozen* and pirate mash-up clothes, and sometimes we'd hold them at the playground while catching our children from the slides. Often we'd Skype after our workouts, both of us looking like sweaty messes. It's just what it takes to be business-owner moms these days, I guess.

"I need more of a lip on the cast-iron skillets," I said as we pushed our littlest blondies in swings.

"Okay," Julia said. "Are you sure? You wanted these to be thin like the old kind."

"I know. But Uncle Doug says too thin will crack easily. We need the extra weight along the rim—Will! Let your sister go down the slide!"

"My girls can take turns with Hannah."

"No, it's fine, they have to share. But seriously—how hard is it to add a bit of thickness?"

"Not too hard." Julia was already processing the steps in her head, cogs visibly turning while she pushed her youngest back and forth. "I think it's easy enough—I have to take him out, he's leaning out of the swing too far."

"Good. I'm glad it's not too trick—Will! Share!"

Those meetings did yield fruit, though, and we sent the designs for a typical 8-inch cast-iron skillet off to Mike, my Wisconsin-based toolmaker. I've met Mike only once, but from what I'd heard from people who knew tooling well, he did a heck of a job. At his shop, Mike made the aluminum tool that would be used to create individual sand molds for every cast-iron pan in my line. (In cast-iron work, there are lots of words used for mold, including *pattern*, *match plate*, *cope and drag*, and *tool* or *tooling*.)

After Mike formed the two aluminum tool plates needed to make a single design, he sent them straight to the foundry for some initial tests and runs—the prototyping stage. It was time for another visit.

The next time I drove the hour and a half up to Roloff Foundry, I wore proper shoes and a flannel work shirt. Julia came along, and when we rang the bell at the foundry, we were so excited to see our cast-iron pans in iron flesh, as it were.

The guys had been hard at work pouring the iron. It takes at least four people to create each cast-iron piece, starting with the person handling the charge in the furnace where the iron is melted and mixed. The molten iron is poured into a large crucible running on a rail throughout the building, which is covered in ceramic cloth and pushed over to the processing machine. At the machine, one person uses Mike's pattern to create identical sand molds while another takes molten iron from the large crucible and puts it into a smaller crucible. He then walks along a slowly moving belt, individually pouring iron into each sand mold. The iron hardens quickly, and a few minutes later the blackened sand falls into the heap at the end of the conveyor belt, with the cast-iron skillet cushioned inside. They did a few trial runs for us, giving us a feel for the tempo.

And there they were! Picking the pans up was wonderful. As we turned them over in our hands, one of the guys mentioned off-handedly that we might want to adjust one part to eliminate breakage. Sure enough, the helper-handle ledge opposite the main handle was extremely thin. How had that managed to slip by the plastic prototype? I'll tell you how: I didn't know what to look for! This meant production had to be pushed back while I spent a few hundred dollars to have Mike reconfigure the aluminum pattern.

While that preproduction was going on at the tool-and-die shop and foundry, late one night I was sitting at home, my children sound asleep, when I had a sudden shocking and horrible realization: The next step after casting iron was seasoning the pans, and I had absolutely no way to get it done! I stared at John, my eyes bugging out and my mouth agape.

"What?" he asked suspiciously.

"Seasoning! *How* are we going to season the pans?"

He seemed perplexed. "Seasoning? Don't they come like that?" (He knew even less about cast iron than I did.)

"No! They come raw! What are we going to do?"

He shrugged and went to our immediate go-to. "Ask your uncle Doug."

So I did, and Uncle Doug assured me I could season them myself if I could get a hot enough fire in the firepit—we'd smoke out the house if we used the kitchen oven. The notion was daunting, but we resigned ourselves to building fires and figuring it out. With that vague idea tucked away, and with the helper-handle problem fixed, I put in an order at Roloff Foundry for fifty skillets.

When the foundry called to let me know the skillets were ready, I borrowed my father-in-law's pickup truck and, with toddler Jack in the backseat, drove down quiet country roads across Wisconsin to pick them up, plus a few burn barrels for seasoning, which the guys kindly gave me.

Dave, the owner of Roloff, asked me a bunch of questions about how I'd be working with the iron and selling it (while he managed to sneak a little candy to Jack).

"I'll sell the cast iron online and in small stores," I explained, wondering how I was going to get a sugar-high kid back in his car seat.

"But everyone makes cast iron," Dave said.

"I know that!" I didn't tell Dave how nervous it made me. I knew there was some stiff competition out there! "But mine will be hand seasoned or raw oiled, so people can season it themselves without having to strip off the original seasoning. No one offers the raw oiled anywhere."

"That's true," Dave agreed. "And it's a classic size. Well, good luck!"

The skillets made it home, and I showed John what we needed to do to season the pans. He responded, "Can we do more research on this? Or at least have some friends come over?"

Guess what? Everyone wanted in on the fire seasoning! Suddenly we had more offers than we knew what to do with. This would have been flattering except that every time John and I built a fire it was trial and error. In fact, we were really awful at building fires! Cardboard starters, ash, and paper went up in heavy gray-white clouds of smoke as we struggled to get a blaze going.

"Why are you building a fire in the middle of the day?" our neighbor, an engineer, asked as he materialized in our yard one spring afternoon. "And in the middle of the backyard?"

I explained why while John continued to fight the flames—or the lack thereof.

"Do you have fire starters?" he asked.

We looked at him like he had five heads. "Fire starters?" We'd kept thinking *old-school pioneer cookware* and had forgotten that we were allowed to use modern inventions to make things easier. Fire starters acquired, and

THE MAKING OF A CAST-IRON PAN

Roloff Foundry, Kaukauna, Wisconsin

1 Patterns (or match plates, tooling, cope and drag . . . there are so many words for the same thing!) are created for the design of any piece of cast iron, which will allow the duplication of the exact same sand casting of a cast-iron piece to be made.

2 These boxes hold the sand, where the shape of the cast-iron casting is held after being formed by the reusable pattern.

3 Sand is used in all cast-iron casting processes, as it will hold the shape of the cast-iron design.

4 The furnace is where the charge happens. In a charging, pig iron, rail iron, and scrap are melted together to form liquid iron.

5

6

5 After the charge from the furnace is emptied into a large mobile crucible, which is hung from rails in the ceiling, some of the slag (impurities) is pulled out, and other additives, like silicon, can be introduced.

6 Then the molten iron is pushed through the foundry to where other foundry workers are pouring individual pieces of cast iron. Pouring can be done by hand, which typically requires six people, or using a processing machine, which needs about half as many people.

7

8

7 The molten iron is poured into a much smaller crucible, which will be used by a single operator to pour the iron into individual prepared molds.

8 Additional impurities are removed if necessary.

9 On a processing machine, a conveyer belt moves molds as an operator walks along the line with a small crucible of molten iron. The iron is poured into each mold and continues along.

10 By the time the cast-iron castings reach the end of the conveyer belt and fall off, the sand is burned black, and the castings, still too hot to touch, are cooled enough that they will hold their shape. The sand busts apart. Using tools, the castings are dug out by hand.

11 Once cooled, the cast-iron pieces are shaken clean. They go to the grinding room, where the gating (the place at which the metal was poured in) is ground and the edges are rounded off.

12 These raw cast-iron pieces are shipped to the customer.

with the neighbor's help, we were able to season a good batch of skillets that very afternoon.

First we heated the skillets completely with three per burn barrel, burning off any water hidden deep within the iron's pores. I wanted to offer different stages of cast-iron cookware: raw oiled and fully seasoned. The first option burns off the microscopic water sitting on and inside the porous iron itself, which happens whenever raw iron hits the air, and then seals in the "dryness" with oil, and that's it. For raw oil seasoning, we simply set them in a 300°F fire (we used a meat thermometer!) for at least 30 minutes, put a thin coat of flaxseed oil all over the pans, and left them to cool. This process keeps rust off the skillets and doesn't require much work for people who want to season the skillets themselves. The skillets look almost naked—quite silver even with the coat of oil. These pans were going to always be a bit sticky, but those who bought them would understand why.

To make fully seasoned pans, we went through the same process as the raw oiled skillet preparation and then we added more wood to the fire and got the temperature up to 500°F to 600°F. We'd take a raw oiled skillet, add a coat of oil, and put it back on the fire, a process we'd repeat six times to achieve a fully seasoned skillet. On our first day we seasoned about fifteen pans, which turned out pretty decently and gave us the confidence to invite more friends over to help with the rest. We were going to have fun!

It was exciting. And hot. As early fall turned into late November, our friends now arrived in fleece and hats. The fires roared—once we'd learned how to build them consistently.

It was so hot, in fact, that the air scorched.

"John," I said, annoyed at the odd little flakes I was brushing from my jacket, "do you need to add more wood to the fire? There are bits of ash coming up again."

He looked up at me. "Ooohoo, Sar . . ." he began, sounding both amused and a little shocked. "You burned the entire end of your braid off."

That got my attention. "Damn." Then I glanced at him. "Um. The front of your hair is burned, too. And parts of your eyebrows."

This prompted a burn check on everyone. Our buddy noticed that his coat had large holes from where he was standing too close to the fire. "Well, it was old," he reasoned. We gave him more beer.

The heat also meant that the cast iron had to be closely monitored, as the oil we were using could heat beyond its smoke point and combust the

Seasoning in any season still gives you lots of smoke!

minute we sprayed it on the skillet. Now *that* was a surprise! Nothing like going *spritz-spritz* and creating a pan full of fire!

Sometimes we season in the bitter cold of a Wisconsin January. On the ice of the backyard, we build fires, fight the weather and the wind, and yes, drink beer with friends while seasoning. I discovered that one can get minor frostbite while wearing steel-toe boots. Whoops!

Still, the fire and the iron (and the beer) always make for a photo-worthy bonding experience. The white puffs of smoke as the oil polymerizes on the surface of the blue-hot metal blow away in our windy backyard, and the burn barrels slowly melt the ice below. The barrels themselves are constantly needing a shim to keep from keeling over unexpectedly. We've even had people who were building their own cast-iron pieces come up for the day to learn to season and share a meal. (It's humbling to be called someone's cookware-building mentor. . . .) Standing over a fire and watching the flames lick along the slowly darkening sides of a skillet strikes that primal place in all our hearts. I love how it brings together friends and family—the process never gets old.

My uncle Carlos and aunt Carol and my parents make dates to come up and try their hand at seasoning on bright, sunny, crisp fall afternoons, when the grass is turning straw-like and runs the risk of combusting.

And the kids always dance too close to the flames.

Collaborating with the foundry, Julia, cast-iron collectors, and Uncle Doug meant I was able to create cast-iron skillets in the model of the old pioneers. I've since learned that it takes a small village (and a lot of time and clement weather) to make the skillets black and shimmery with seasoning. It's like anything else: Dive in and learn and you'll reap the benefits.

Though iron's history is steeped in warfare, it has become a staple for the making of sturdy, heavy cookware that handles heat differently from the other kitchen staples, copper and clay. It is historical as well as modern, beloved even when it requires work to keep it in operation. When it's well crafted and cared for, it can become heirloom cookware, too. And while we all know what cast-iron cookware looks like, it can still be an enigmatic kitchen tool for some and the center of a debate for others. For instance, the seasoning process is key to the longevity of cast iron, but there is a robust and hearty ongoing argument among makers and lovers of cast iron about the best way to accomplish a solid season. Cast iron has its own cult-like following, with whole dues-paying associations and groups dedicated to the documentation, use, care, and collecting of it. Cast iron is even more of a cookware staple these days than copper, so a book on heirloom cookware wouldn't be complete without a history lesson about it. Let's dive into the fire!

IRON AND US

Unsurprisingly, iron's use in culture has no exact discovery date. It exists all over the world in various forms and oxides, both close to the surface and below it, but never free and clear by itself. Iron bonds with other naturally occurring elements such as carbon and minerals like hematite. As with copper, its properties were discovered slowly in disparate cultures across the globe, as people became smarter . . . or at least learned more about fire! As with all metals, iron was first worked to make killer (pun intended) weapons, so your army might have an advantage over the neighboring one.

Imagine bearing down on your foes with soft copper shields and spearheads, only to be matched with crazy-eyed opponents wielding iron swords and breastplates that bend your weapons like they were made of butter! So it was with iron upon its first serious use.

It's hard to say which culture was the first to discover that a hot-enough fire would allow iron to bend, break, twist, or melt. It certainly was a gigantic leap for mankind to be able to manipulate a substance that created such a strong finished product. Copper, bronze, and brass are pretty soft by comparison, and iron may have been more brittle, but this trait was offset by its weight, perceived strength, and ability to withstand a much harder and longer beating.

And it's fun to imagine the upper-body strength that came along with blacksmithing all that iron. But this book isn't called *Copper, Iron, and Clay: Our Love Affair with Muscle-Bound Blacksmiths*, so I'll leave it at that.

The Hittites in Asia Minor (and, depending whom you're talking to, people from Cyprus) are credited by most archaeologists with fine-tuning the metallurgic science required to mass-produce iron. The Hittites valued this metal as something almost magical and worked hard to discover its most useful properties. One of their kings, sitting on his mountaintop "Iron Throne" in Hattusa, or modern-day Turkey (I knew I'd get one *Game of Thrones* reference in), wrote to another monarch that he was sending along a small iron weapon as a gift but, alas, could not send "good iron" to share otherwise. The Hittites probably wished to keep their knowledge secret and maintain the advantage of higher-quality weapons. Eventually the Hittite Empire died out, but archaeologists believe that their metalsmiths shared their ironworking know-how as they dispersed among other cultures. It's thought that these smiths were elevated to the same high status enjoyed by coppersmiths of the period.

At the same time, the island of Cyprus possessed huge deposits of ochre and umber (two great natural sources of iron ore), and the Cypriots rivaled the Hittites in their ability to experiment and forge the finest iron. Excavations in the late 1990s support the theory that renowned metallurgists on the island would have had both the wherewithal and knowledge to test any accidentally produced high-quality iron, even if that happened fairly seldom. Most of the finished Cyprus-made cast iron would have been exceedingly brittle, which means (no shock!) that they focused on making swords, which were great for their time but could still shatter with a heavy blow. (Those early swords had nothing on the later models forged in steel.)

The blacksmith trade as we know it now began about thirty-five hundred years ago, although primitive furnaces were seldom hot enough to extract iron effectively from ore. Even if a high temperature could be reached for a short period of time to allow someone to start separating the grime, dirt, and unwanted elements from the pure iron molecules, the iron would still be left with impurities. The poor quality of this metal would "fail" during any forging work, cracking, breaking, or simply not heating well enough for proper ironworking—like making swords that didn't shatter! The problems with purifying iron ore made iron a rare and expensive commodity that was exceedingly difficult to procure in large quantities. Thus, the oldest iron items found have been small rings and spearheads, pieces made for warfare and battle that could be reused by another soldier. A home three thousand years ago would contain few or no iron items, and certainly not a big iron cooking pot.

The refining process for iron remained consistent for several hundred years, and during those centuries, the process always required the work of large, sturdy men called puddlers. These men needed incredible stamina because they stood near the heat for hours, where they'd draw off the slag and debris and then the iron itself while stirring the liquefied metal. Once purer iron was produced as "iron blooms" pulled off by puddlers, those brawny smiths would pound, heat, and compact the metal to create wrought iron. This little-remembered job is an important slice of ironworking history. The insane difficulty of the work meant that puddlers usually died very young for their time.

Prior to the invention of the blast furnace, in which cast iron could be melted in hotter temperatures than the fires the ancient smiths could create, iron was used almost exclusively for warfare items and knives. With better tools, hotter fire, and a growing understanding of oxygen and carbon levels, iron could be beaten and hammered into thinner pieces that were tough enough to handle bending but still very strong. Suddenly, iron cookware was a possibility. The first iron pots were slim pieces heated, hammered, and sometimes riveted together (using nails), unlike the solid pieces we see today.

Some of the older iron pots found by archaeologists were discovered in the Mosfell valley, a few miles outside Reykjavik, Iceland, and date back to the traditional Viking Age (the site is dated from approximately 790 to 1100 CE). A fragment from a small iron pot, estimated at only 7 $\frac{1}{2}$ inches in diameter when whole, turned up on a late ninth-century farmstead. The fragment shows how the iron pot was pieced together with at least two iron sheets and then welded together with a loop riveted to the top, allowing the pot to be suspended over fires.

HOW DID THEY DO THAT? EARLY CAST-IRON PROCESS

Like copper and brass of earlier times, the first iron cookware molds were created using the "lost wax" process (see page 56). American smiths then moved to "loam-molding" cast iron in the mid-1600s, because it was less labor intensive and more predictable than lost wax. In loam-molding, a smith would wind a cord around a spindle until the shape of the interior of the desired pot was created. The shape was covered with clay and placed against a wood template, which formed a core, allowing for the hollow interior of the pot. After the clay was baked and dusted with charcoal, a second layer of clay was applied and shaped by rotating the piece. A third layer was also added, but not baked, so once semidry, it could be split into two halves, or "cheeks." This third outer layer was used to attach the patterns for any feet or ear handles, and everything was baked again. The middle layer of clay was cracked out, and the third outer layer was reassembled. The space between the first and third layers was held open using little metal pieces called "chaplets," which determined thickness. The spindle was drawn out, and the holes from it were plugged in the first and second layers; the last, outer layer became the open "gate" to let the molten metal in. The entire mold was buried in the earth to be held together against the hot metal, and then the hot metal was poured in. When the whole thing was cool, you'd dig it out and have a cast-iron pot!

INTERVIEW WITH DOUG MERKEL, RENOWNED TRADITIONAL BLACKSMITH, RETIRED OWNER OF BEAR MOUNTAIN FORGE, AND MY AMAZING UNCLE

Uncle Doug passed away at the end of March 2019, and I miss him! I keep thinking he is only an email away . . .

What tools did blacksmiths use five hundred years ago that are still used today?
Well, you still need anvils, though they've changed in shape. Now they're made of steel instead of wrought iron with a steel plate on top. Hammers haven't changed, and neither have blacksmith tongs. Now, though, a blacksmith can use water-powered hammers or air or electric ones. [These make the job easy and allow for more work to be done in the same amount of time!] But you're still squashing metal.

How is wrought iron different from cast iron?
Wrought iron is almost pure iron but has some slag in the form of filaments. Wrought is a malleable form of iron. *Wrought* can also be a verb, meaning something is handmade, whereas simply *wrought iron* refers to a type of iron. Cast iron, on the other hand, has 1.5 to 4 percent carbon in it, so it's a brittle alloy of iron and carbon combined. It's hard and readily cast.

How are forges and foundries different?
First of all, a forge is a place as well as a verb. So, you visit a forge, where a blacksmith works, but you can also forge metal. For instance, to forge is to make an item with heat, anvil, and hammer. A foundry is a workshop for melting and casting metal into molds. But back in the day, foundries were called bloomeries. They made blooms of iron that were fished out and hammered, becoming wrought iron.

You know, there were lots of ways blacksmiths worked on iron in those forges and foundries. They'd make "blister steel" in Europe, which was layers of wrought iron compacted with layers of bones that acted as carbon. Those layers were heated for days, the carbon would burn off, and you'd end up with a one-thirty-second inch of steel on the outside and wrought iron on the inside. [You were sandwiching steel inside wrought iron, which was the way they could make steel without all our fancy machines.] Then they'd stack and heat those good pieces of blister steel, and that would create "sheer steel," which was obviously hard to make, so it was really expensive. [Unsurprisingly, this type of steel was a favorite for knives and swords and not cooking pots!]

What is it about blacksmithing that appeals to you?

The material itself speaks to me. How it works, how it becomes what you want it to become. So many people, when they're just learning, think, *Oh! I'm going to wreck it!* But so what? You can't really mess it up. You can put life into the metal. Only you can feel what it wants to be, only you can do it. It sounds silly, but it's true.

How are blacksmiths active today compared to the past? Do they make cookware?

Blacksmiths make fewer pots and pans today, but they still can. They also make forks, spoons, ladles, meat forks, rotisserie spits, bottle jacks, and clock jacks. It should also be noted that there are a lot of blacksmiths who make only one thing, very refined and very specific. Back in the day, even in small towns of a few thousand people, you might find upward of eighty blacksmiths, with maybe six master smiths among them, all specialized in certain items. The rest did just small agricultural repairs; it used to be that 99 percent of farmers were able to do their own repairs. Overall, though, the time of the blacksmith has evolved and mostly disappeared.

Iron Terminology

Cast iron comes in a variety of grades and mixes, each with its own metallurgic properties best suited for certain activities. The internal structure of the different molecules inside the cast iron makes the iron behave differently when heated: Hence, gray cast-iron handles were too brittle for my copper pots, but ductile iron worked just fine during the riveting and tinning. Want to know the differences in short? Here you go:

Cast Iron: Made of reduced iron ore, it has a wide range of carbon content, from 1.5 percent to more than 4 percent. Cast iron is combined with manganese and silicon during heating. It is quite brittle because the graphite within the cast iron is flat and shard-like. Cast iron cracks and chips easily.

Ductile Iron: Rarely used in cookware except as handles or as a less expensive version of carbon steel (see below), ductile iron is extremely strong and much more malleable and less brittle than cast iron due to the graphite molecule structure within the iron being round, which is done during the melting process by adding magnesium. Also made of reduced iron ore, ductile iron has a very tight, specific carbon content of 3.1 to 3.6 percent. Copper or tin can be added in minute amounts to make it stronger and less likely to corrode.

Cast or Carbon Steel: This metal contains less than 0.5 percent carbon. It's by far the most expensive iron currently in casting production, because it's more finicky to cast and results in more waste, but it's prized for its corrosion resistance and is even more of a "bendy" iron than ductile. Because it expands faster when heated and is so much more anti-corrosive than other irons, it's now more commonly used in modern cookware.

As technology advanced, with the invention of steam power and then, a bit later, the Industrial Revolution, a large chunk of the manual labor previously required throughout the casting process was eliminated, and high-quality iron became readily available at a lower price. This led to the creation of cooking pots and pans that look similar to our modern ones.

One of the major advances in cast-iron creation was the widespread use of the blast furnace. These furnaces are vertical structures in which suitable heat is maintained to allow intense combustion (the perfect fire!) by blasting air into alternating layers of charcoal (and, later, coke), flux (crushed seashells or limestone), and iron ore. A blast furnace can process (make purer) many different metals from copper to lead to iron, but its initial invention was mainly for the purpose of creating different irons, the most common being pig iron, a rough ingredient for creating cast iron. The iron running off a blast furnace can be poured into molds depending on what you're making—pig iron mix is poured into ingot shapes for easier transport and later melting, whereas purer cast iron is put into more familiar cookware molds, for instance.

The blast furnace was developed from smaller furnaces dating back to Roman times and grew in size over the centuries. They appeared during the Middle Ages in western Europe, but archaeological evidence points to these furnaces being invented separately in China and Africa, too, at a slightly earlier time, though the dates are uncertain. France and Belgium operated the furnaces as early as the mid-twelfth century, and the casting of iron pots quickly became lucrative if you had enough funds to build a furnace and pay workers. Additionally, once the smiths understood how to make curved and hollowed pieces for—you guessed it—warfare items like cannons, these skills also allowed for numerous new styles of pots for kitchens.

Then, in 1707, Englishman Andrew Darby revealed his sand-casting innovation, which allowed for a design to be made in sand forms so that a single design could be made over and over very efficiently. Sand-casting had been tinkered with as early as the 1540s, but Darby's methods could be replicated without too many explosively unexpected results. No more "breaking the mold," as was needed with wax casting. Darby's patented process revolutionized cast iron, which became inexpensive, quick to produce, and available to all income levels. Iron began to be cast from pig iron and leftover scrap iron (basically the castoffs from castings that didn't look nice or broke) in larger and larger quantities. The cooking landscape changed again.

Shortly after Darby's patent took off, blast furnaces were largely replaced by cupola furnaces, which used the same combination of charcoal (and coke in later years), limestone, air, and iron ore, but the big difference was that they could be heated constantly, melting iron at a much more rapid pace and allowing for even greater production of cast-iron goods. Blast furnaces continued to create the more rudimentary pig iron for blacksmith forges for wrought iron, but pig iron was also handed off to cupola furnaces.

For the next 120 years after the sand-casting invention and use of the more productive cupola furnaces, the technology for cast-iron cookware essentially stayed the same, though aesthetics evolved. Then, after World War II ended in 1945, electric furnaces were all the rage, and foundries made the switch over en masse. Electric furnaces are the standard in today's metalworking facilities.

WHY COOK IN CAST IRON?

It's pretty! It's nonstick if seasoned properly! It holds heat evenly a long time once you get it hot! It can go on the stove, in the oven, and over fire! (These last things apply to copper as well, but who's keeping score?) Cast-iron users and collectors are by far the most opinionated group of cookware mavens I've ever met, and they're likely to break into heated discussion about the merits of different fats and oils for seasoning, the temperature at which to season, the method for making the interior smooth, or the history and prominence of various now-defunct makers.

But what's really special about cast iron? To start, it's important to understand how cast iron's molecular makeup reacts to heat.

When heated, the molecules in cast iron don't move very fast. They don't conduct heat quickly, and that means heat doesn't pass through the graphite structures of the material with the same ease as copper, tin, aluminum, and silver. Remember when I said that copper heats twenty-five times

faster than stainless steel? Copper conducts heat about seven times faster than cast iron. A heat source on cast iron, like a flame, works its way slowly and unevenly through the material, which is why you often hear of cast-iron pans having hot spots. These are caused by the molecular structure of the iron, which creates extremely hard, dense, flake-like shapes within the graphite. These shapes are also why you hear people call cast iron "brittle."

I ran into this issue myself when the first round of cast-iron handles I had made for my copper cookware were gray iron instead of ductile. The handles cracked constantly, whether it was during the riveting or tinning process. The gray cast iron was just not malleable enough.

When you're actually using cast iron as intended, the issue of hot spots becomes moot, because you should always get the iron hot through and through, all the way down the handle (until it's too hot to touch without a pad), before adding food. The biggest beauty of cast-iron performance, after all, is its ability to hold on to heat. So first get the iron really hot, and *then* you have a uniform heat source for cooking your food.

There's something to be said for the even, uniform, long-lasting surround of warmth for cooking. It's why a Dutch oven was so treasured by pioneers snuggled in sod homesteads, colonial Americans, and anyone who likes a good pie, for instance: It held coals on its top, effectively creating an oven by using those coals to evenly heat the air and surrounding metal and cook the food inside. The same principle holds true whether you're cooking on a cast-iron griddle or a deep-frying skillet. Once the iron is hot, it will stay hot for a long time after you remove it from the flame. This feature allows you to slowly cook or bake, or to place it in your oven to keep warm without using a lot of energy. Cast iron, for all its mechanical brittleness, is a pretty hardy piece of cookware to have in your house and, like copper, will last many generations if you take care of it.

Cast iron is heirloom cookware, of course, because it can be passed from parent to child. And while cast iron will rust if not properly cared for (left to rust, over decades it will fall apart into red flakes), if you wash it appropriately and season it well, it is no more difficult to care for than copper. I firmly believe that any pure metal cookware is worth the bit of hand-washing and occasional polishing or seasoning to keep it up and running.

As any home cook with a decent array of pots and pans will know, there are certain metals and materials chosen to cook certain foods. Cast iron probably offers the most options in terms of use, so it's the closest thing to heirloom "anything goes" cookware. You can bake in it, so brownies, corn bread, and fruit crumble can all go in your high-walled skillet and into the oven. Just be aware that cast iron will heat and cook differently from ceramic or aluminum bakeware. If you follow the exact timing given in a baking recipe without heating the pan first, cold spots will affect your recipe, likely causing it to be undercooked. To avoid this, I throw the cast iron into the preheating oven while I mix a batter; this way, I'll know that the iron is properly heated before I pour in the batter. Another way to deal with the cold spots is to bake a recipe a bit longer than the time specified, checking every few minutes until it's baked through.

Beyond baking delicious desserts and breads, though, cast iron is fantastic for searing meat, grilling burgers and cheese sandwiches, and deep-frying chicken. Throw bacon and eggs in the same pan together or separately and they both cook perfectly on a well-seasoned iron bottom. Truly, cast iron is great for nearly anything. So if you have a few sizes, you'll be set.

WHEN NOT TO USE CAST IRON

This one is easy: Don't use it for any dishes that require exact heat. Why? For the very same reason it's great for baking and slow cooking and frying: Cast iron holds heat a *looooong* time. So if you're planning to make a fancy béchamel sauce, don't use cast iron. If you want extreme control over the temperature at which your ingredients simmer, don't use cast iron. The heat will stay in the pan long after you've turned off the burner, which can result in overcooking, scalding, and even burning.

Cooking in cast iron over an open fire is thrilling every time!

INTERVIEW WITH MARY SUE MILLIKEN,

CHEF, AUTHOR, ENTREPRENEUR, AND A *TOP CHEF MASTERS* WINNER

It's a small world. John was talking to his childhood friend about my crazy cookware business, and his buddy said something like, "Hey, I have a family friend who is a chef. I guess she's kind of a big deal." Suddenly I had Mary Sue's contact information. Turns out Wisconsin connections go far. See more on Mary Sue, plus her recipe for Rhubarb Pie, on page 230!

What does the term *heirloom cookware* mean to you?

I think of Granny—my kid's great-grandma, who loved to cook and would go to those junkyard sales and find old Americana. She had lots of old things like cast iron and a Bundt pan made of clay. The term reminds me of cooking with love and of an era when life was slower.

How important do you believe the relationship is among food, chef, cookware, and recipient?

I think of food as the raw material put into a gentler atmosphere when you're using older cooking techniques, and when you're using old pots and pans, so the chef doesn't have to be as involved. If you are using inferior cookware, you'll notice a huge difference in performance. I can cook over a campfire with a butter knife. I'm not a fancy cookware person, but I see the wisdom in using all the old cookware because it makes cooking a lot easier. For instance, if your oven is kind of "scorch," or has a tendency to burn things, then the food won't cook right if you have flimsy cookware. But if you cook in a ceramic coffee cup in the same scorchy oven, it will be gentler on the food, because the heat is transferred the way it should be.

Why do chefs love certain cookware?

It's comfort. Habit. Cooking is repetitive. Along with your raw materials or food and equipment, you get a rhythm. You have a chance to pay close attention to the tiniest details. But if you change something in the equation—different cookware thickness or shape—then you have a new set of challenges. So you start to trust your cookware and tools. You know how they will cook and work, so it frees you up mentally. You can be more creative, and you know what to expect.

What is your favorite piece?

At home, I use sauté pans all the time. Just having a good, solid, thick, heavy, high-quality sauté pan is great for quick dinners. And I also like to make crispy rice in cast iron. The cast iron forms a crust with the rice that is just right and crunchy. I have had favorites over the years, but I also have been forced to be pretty flexible because I cook all over the world, and sometimes I don't have the exact thing I want.

How do you believe cookware affects the culinary landscape?

I think trends in cookware are important because they provide a unique outlet for creative energy and looking at things anew. Whatever the trend might be, whether toward heirloom wares or immersion circulators, it matters because it opens horizons. People get to try things out, and the really solid things stick and stay and become part of culinary traditions. And America is still so young, it's great we have this experimentation going on with ingredients, ways of cooking, and different cookware. For instance, right now there's a whole movement of going back and cooking with fire, and at the same time, we're looking at cooking in vacuum bags. It's all exciting.

What's the most important action in a piece of cookware?

Performance is key for me, because if I take care of everything and respect it, I don't have to replace it. Sustainability and performance are the most important, equally.

Do they teach the science of cookware in culinary school?

When I apprenticed in France, I learned from the chefs over there. I was taught about copper being the best thing to whip egg whites in, and we had copper bowls for that purpose . . . but it was scratching the surface in terms of cookware science. For the most part, commercial kitchens are not about the cookware, except point five percent. The majority are inhabited with cheap aluminum cookware because of skinny margins, and you just don't have a chance to cook in the slow way that you would if you were in a three-star restaurant in France.

As a groundbreaker in the culinary field and changing the rules at times, what do you think is the next culinary challenge to overcome?

Especially in America, we have such a luxury of diversity in our culture. We get to eat all the food connected to that diversity, but some of it is marginalized and not really given recognition. I think we are starting to do that more, while looking at diversity of gender, race, ethnicity, in everything we do. It's going to be an important piece going ahead.

I get asked a lot about what standard ironware to include in a fully stocked kitchen. First, you can collect vintage pieces for everyday use, or you can buy them new. Some people treasure the silky smoothness of old iron poured with fine sand and smoothed by time and age and use. Others like to experience different variations in cast iron by trying cast-steel pans. Know that the finish (smooth or rough) doesn't actually affect the way the molecules of the iron behave when heated; cast iron works the same whatever its cooking surface. You may find yourself bitten with the collector's bug as you start to stock your shelves with black iron, or maybe not. Either way, make sure it's seasoned and ready before you throw in food.

The Skillet or Frying Pan

A skillet (or frying pan) will have straight sides that flare out only slightly from bottom to top. A vintage pan may have three legs under it, but a modern one won't. A long handle on a very heavy skillet will usually be paired with either a short handle or helper ledge on the opposite end. Old skillets will usually be completely round, whereas modern skillets may have one or more pouring spouts along the edge. You can use cast-iron skillets for everything from frying eggs to searing steaks to baking brownies. It's the most versatile iron cookware piece and comes in a dizzying array of sizes and shapes. For starters, find good 8-inch, 10-inch, and 12-inch round skillets and play from there!

The Pot

Cast-iron pots were traditionally round bodied, and vintage ones have three legs. In contrast with kettles (below), which get wider at the top, pots get narrower. The pots would have hung over hearth fires or campfires but today are excellent for making soup, or for boiling sausages before throwing them on the grill. Most pots now are considered vintage, even if they were made well into the 1900s.

The Kettle

You're likely going to find a Dutch oven before you find a kettle, because kettles under the traditional definition aren't made anymore. Vintage kettles will have legs, but anything that has straight sides and is relatively deep/tall is considered a kettle. If you have a kettle, you can forgo buying a Dutch oven, and vice versa. Unlike a Dutch oven, however, a kettle traditionally does not have a lid.

The Dutch Oven

Why is it called an oven? Because you can settle it into a fire, pop on the lid, and pile ashes on the top, cooking on all sides of the pan and creating an "oven" effect. Dutch ovens are usually slightly deeper than skillets (vintage ovens also have tiny legs on the bottom) and always sell with a lid, as the lid is what makes the piece an oven at all. Le Creuset is the famous current maker of the enameled version of a Dutch oven. Also use the Dutch oven for anything you would normally use a big stainless-steel pot for—boiling water for pasta, for instance.

The Griddle

This is a multipurpose kitchen tool if ever there was one! Flat, with or without an outer-rim lip, the griddle sits comfortably on a stovetop or in an oven. You may choose from a variety of shapes—square, round, or rectangular—and opt for a handle or not. Griddles are great for everything from frying pancakes to pizza to tortillas to hamburgers, but because they lack sides, griddle cooking can be messy, so be prepared to do a thorough wipe-down around your stove after you've used it.

The Scotch Bowl

Unfortunately, no one makes Scotch bowls anymore, but if there's enough demand, perhaps someone will! Happily, they are relatively easy to find online or from used-goods stores and resale shops. Scotch bowls are rounded along the bottom, making them perfect for soups, stir-fries, and even oatmeal (cooking daily porridge was their original use!) and are a great addition to the kitchen menagerie for the collector and aficionado alike.

The Muffin Pan

You can find both vintage and modern muffin pans (sometimes called cake pans) for making small items from cupcakes to corn bread. They come with flat or round bottoms and in rectangular or circular shapes. Muffin pans should be treated and seasoned like other cast-iron pans. This can be time consuming, but otherwise they will rust. You can reduce the cleaning and care time by using cupcake wrappers in the individual wells, whether you're making muffins or mini meat loaves!

The Lid

Though some manufacturers make glass and plastic lids for their cast-iron wares, I strongly recommend investing in a solid iron lid in the size or two of your most commonly used skillets. First, they will last longer: Glass tends to break, and it will scratch against the cast iron, too. Cast-iron lids will hold in the heat properly. Plus, the handles will not pop off, as they are also made of iron, and all the metal will heat and cool together without slowly wiggling apart, as can happen with mismatched metals (such as aluminum or bronze handles screwed onto a cast-iron lid). If you purchase the lid and cookware from separate manufacturers, be sure the interior lip of the cover will fit neatly within the pan body to avoid a wobbling lid.

The Fun Piece

This may be a vintage find you snatch at a garage sale or flea market, or if you join the Griswold and Cast Iron Cookware Association, you'll get an insider's pick at auctions and swaps. You may hunt for a two-sided waffle iron, a Danish cake pan, or a domed broiler lid. Or perhaps you'll go for something modern. Thanks to the renaissance of cast iron, there are many boutique foundries pouring specialty shapes, including the fifty states, unique tree-shape handles, or hexagonal bodies. These are usable, of course, but also show pieces—great for sitting out on the stove, hanging from your pan rack, or displaying dinner party recipes. You might consider these your serving pieces more than your everyday workhorses, but they are just as effective as the basic ones for cooking and baking.

THE GRISWOLD AND CAST IRON COOKWARE ASSOCIATION

When someone is just getting started with collecting cast iron, what are the key pieces they should look for?

Most collectors begin their collections with one or more items that were handed down to them from a relative. These pieces have a sentimental value because they remember the cooked meals that came out of them and who made them. When these collectors then start adding to these inherited pieces, they try to buy every piece of cast-iron cookware that they can find. Most will buy the same brand, but the few that don't will buy any iron they see for sale. I know because I've done that. For new collectors, I would suggest buying pieces they like. If you're buying to make a usable collection, buy pieces that are not cracked, pitted, or missing parts like lids or bail (bucket-style) handles. If you're buying only to display, look for pieces that are as close to new as possible, or ornate and unusual.

What are the hallmarks of a good "find" or a vintage piece in good or excellent condition?

A good find, to a collector, is a piece that still has the label in it, or pans that still have the swirl grind marks from the original grinding and/or polishing process from manufacturing. There are many collectors who look for pans that have a patina from extensive use and smoke rings that are worn down from sliding on wood-stove tops for many years. Some collectors look for pans that have had repairs in their lifetime.

Advanced collectors should be experts in the area they're collecting; they should be passionate and learn all they can in the area of their expertise and pass that information on to all who will listen. For instance, I still actively collect cast-iron cookware, but my passion is cast-iron mailboxes; I have more than one hundred fifty different ones. I always have a photo book of my collection to show at conventions, and I receive many messages from other collectors seeking answers to questions about cast mailboxes.

What kinds of networks are available for collectors?

There are a couple of collectors' clubs—Griswold and Cast Iron Cookware Association and the Wagner and Griswold Society—and also many Facebook pages dedicated to collectors of cast-iron cookware. Many advanced collectors are more than willing to pass on information to anyone who asks.

The clubs have national meets every year at which they hold seminars dedicated to specialized areas of collecting. There are show-and-tell events for individuals to bring their unusual pieces. These clubs also have regional meets. You can also use one of the many books dedicated to cast-iron collecting.

Seasoning cast iron can be intimidating. So some makers decided to fix that. Welcome to the next piece of technology: enamel!

To continue manufacturing cast iron but to appeal to people who worried about the care of the seasoning and who just didn't have as much time to spend in the kitchen anymore, several companies started to create other kinds of cast-iron cookware, from the ceramic to the enameled.

Enameled cast iron is not made to last. Once it starts to chip, it will rust unless seasoning is performed to those small spots—an unlikely and sometimes impossible task unless one tries to season the entire interior of the enameled cookware. Since many people do not wish to have "dirty"-looking cookware, they allow the raw iron to be exposed to air, resulting in additional chipping and brittleness as well as rusting. Then they toss it. But you don't have to! If your enameled cast iron starts to chip, try to season it using the same methods you would if you had a bare piece of ironware. If that's not possible, continue using it until rust grows on it—as long as the enamel isn't chipping off into your food.

SEASONING CAST IRON

Oh, the never-ending question: *How to season a cast-iron skillet?* Many cast-iron cookbooks have expounded on this question over the years, and I don't think we're any closer to a general consensus. Chefs who are experts in a wide variety of cuisines have offered opinions on the various chemical and natural ways to season cast iron. But the most important factor in choosing your seasoning process is knowing the starting point of your cast iron. The advice that follows is compiled from innumerable sources, including the occasional chat with my blacksmith uncle and other makers around the country, and tested on my own oven and stove or over open fires in the backyard.

Raw Cast Iron

You'll know your cast iron is raw because it's silvery, but you won't often find it available for sale. Raw cast iron is fully porous and fully exposed to the elements, so left untreated it will start to develop rust in about thirty days if exposed to the air. Why? Because of the water in the air! To properly season your piece, you must heat the entire hunk of iron to the boiling point of water (212°F) to essentially "dry out" your ironware.

To season raw iron, you'll need to make several decisions ahead of time, so I've listed out the pros and cons in the chart on pages 140–41.

Preseasoned Cast Iron

If you own or purchase a preseasoned cast-iron piece that already performs (it's not sticky and your eggs slide right off!) the way you like, then you just need to keep maintaining it. This is simple and becomes a soothing routine—another one of those slightly vintage to-dos. You know . . . like washing dishes by hand rather than popping them in a dishwasher!

You'll still need to decide what oil or fat you wish to use for your upkeep based on the pros and cons noted below, as even with a preseasoned skillet there is upkeep as time goes on. The following chart lists a few additional oils to explore. The best part? You could start with one seasoning and switch to another whenever you wish.

For sealing against the elements for long periods of time, I recommend (as did my blacksmith uncle) using food-grade wax. It is imperative that the iron is at 250°F for 15 minutes before you put on the wax so that moisture isn't trapped under it, but the wax will certainly protect any cast-iron or steel cookware for decades. When you want to use the piece again, stick the iron piece in the oven on a top rack with a baking sheet on the bottom rack or tin foil along the bottom. Turn the oven on to 250°F. Check often by wiping a paper towel over the surface of the iron; when the wax starts to come off as liquid, you can remove the whole thing and quickly wipe off as much of the wax as possible. You will probably want to season the iron again with a few coats of your preferred seasoning before using it. This process can be done over a fire, but you won't have as much control over the temperature, of course, so the checking for wiping will be a bit more trial and error.

STRIPPING AND CLEANING PRESEASONED OR VINTAGE (OR YUCKY AND RUSTED) IRONWARE

You'll need to strip your iron pieces if they've been preseasoned with something you don't like. For instance, people with a soy allergy in the family will likely want to strip their commercially purchased skillets to remove

SEASONING FACTOR	PROS	CONS
USING AN OVEN	Can do in your home Can control exact temperature Can do at any time and take breaks easily Is safe (no open fire)	Can be a slow process, taking anywhere from 6 to 10 hours to fully season Takes a lot of heat energy Can smoke up your house Can blacken/make your oven very dirty
USING AN OPEN FIRE	Can do in your backyard over any firepit Is energy efficient Makes no mess in your house/oven Is a very fast process (can do 6 coats in 1 hour)	Requires a contained firepit Less control of temperature Requires planning ahead Requires several coats of a preferred oil to be applied quickly
SEASONING WITH OLIVE OR VEGETABLE OIL	Is inexpensive Has a medium smoke point but does not oxidize ("stick") to the iron as quickly and as effectively as other oils, such as flaxseed Is food safe	Typically contains soy (an allergen) and/or chemicals Can go rancid if not applied correctly or if ironware is not used often Can remain tacky for a long time
SEASONING WITH FLAXSEED OIL	Bonds to the iron quickly through oxidation (and heat) due to its high content of alpha-linolenic acid Is food safe Does not go rancid Does not contain allergens such as soy	Can be more expensive than other oils Has a lower smoke point than other oils and therefore can fill your oven and kitchen with smoke easier than other oils
SEASONING WITH LARD	Is a traditional seasoning Does not typically contain soy or other allergens	Can go rancid if not applied correctly or if ironware is not used often Can remain tacky for a long time
SEASONING LIGHTLY (LESS THAN 6 COATS) WITH ANY OF THE ABOVE	Allows for slow seasoning with food as you use it Takes less initial time to season Reduces chance of improper buildup while seasoning Reduces chance of oil getting too thick and causing drips	Stays "sticky," causing food to stick over many uses, until the seasoning builds up Increases risk of rusting
SEASONING HEAVILY (6 OR MORE COATS) WITH ANY OF THE ABOVE	Is more easily kept up after first use and beyond Will not rust easily	Takes longer to season in the first round Can get drippy/thick and not stick properly if seasoning is hurried

SEASONING FACTOR	PROS	CONS
GRAPESEED OIL	Is easy to find and is inexpensive	Takes longer to become nonstick and shiny Can go rancid if not applied properly and the iron piece is not used often
UNSATURATED BEAR FAT	Creates an authentic seasoning and gets nonstick fast Is great for vintage pieces as it's authentic!	Is very messy to apply and somewhat hard to find Can build up fast and get tacky Can go rancid if not applied properly and the iron piece is not used often
UNSATURATED PIG FAT	Creates an authentic seasoning and becomes nonstick fast Is easier to find than bear fat	Is very messy to apply and somewhat hard to find Can build up fast and get tacky Can go rancid if not applied properly and the iron piece is not used often
REFINED COCONUT OIL	Is easy to find Is great for people who prefer a nonsoy, organic option	Can go rancid if not applied properly and the iron piece is not used often
BACON GREASE	Is easy to find or make Can be used in the pan immediately after frying up bacon in it!	Has lingering bacon smell for a long time after seasoning Must make new bacon grease anytime you want to season Can be messy to apply Can go rancid if not applied properly and the iron piece is not used often
SESAME OIL	Has a higher smoke point than many oils so lessens the chance of fire if the pan gets too hot during seasoning Is readily available and inexpensive	Takes longer to become nonstick and shiny

the preapplied vegetable/soy blend, which you must assume is on any pan that doesn't offer a full list of ingredients used during seasoning in the factory. If you keep kosher, you might want to clean off any original seasoning and start from scratch using kosher oil. You also need to strip or prepare vintage iron if it's rusty or very dirty.

There are divided camps about stripping methods (everyone likes to believe their way is the best . . . and they may be right!). I'll describe both natural and chemical processes below, and you can choose which method works best for your cookware, whether new or vintage.

Natural Stripping

If you want to keep it as natural and organic a process as possible, you can certainly use nonchemical processes to work on your cast iron.

Oven Heat

Invert and place your ironware on top of a ceramic mug (it can sustain the high temperature) to save your nice oven racks and put it into your oven. Turn on the self-cleaning setting. By the end of the cycle, the rust should be burned to ash. Using a hot pad (or two), remove the iron piece an hour or two after the oven shuts off. It'll look gray and ashy.

Wash with warm water, and then immediately return the iron to a warm oven to fully dry. Once dry, season the ironware with a few coats of your preferred oil, returning the iron to the oven in between each coat of oil for full polymerization. Heads up! Do not allow any water, not even one tiny droplet, to sit on the iron or you'll see early superficial rust blooms return quickly, and you'll have to start the process all over again. You may want to have a long TV series to binge-watch standing by!

Fire Heat

Head outside and build a typical wood bonfire or campfire, taking the usual safety precautions of wearing welding gloves, eye safety glasses, and covered shoes. (I learned that wearing steel-toe boots is great. Unless it's January in Wisconsin, which is a great way to court frostbite, regardless of how much beer is available. Another tip!) When you have high flames, place the ironware into the fire and leave it there until the rust has burned off and turned to ash. This can take 1 to 2 hours, depending on how hot your fire is.

Wash it with warm water and put it back on the fire to dry. Once dry, season the ironware with a few coats of your preferred oil. Since you already should have a roaring fire, this will be a natural and easy next step, and will move along quickly as you apply each coat of oil and return it to the fire after each application. Again, do not allow any water, not even one tiny droplet, to sit on the iron.

This is in the kitchen of my friends Barbara Joosse and Chuck Whitehouse. You can see both old and new cast iron, including lots of enameled pieces. Note the repaired skillet *(front far left)* with the welded-on handle.

Vinegar

In a large bucket in which your iron piece can be submerged completely, combine 50 percent distilled white vinegar and 50 percent water (so, for example, a gallon of each for a large piece of ironware). Place your ironware in the bucket to soak until the red rust has flaked off. This can take anywhere from 30 minutes to 6 hours, depending on the breadth and depth of the rust. Check on the piece every 30 minutes, and do not leave it in the solution overnight.

While the iron is still moist from the vinegar bath, scrub it all over with an abrasive material, such as dense rock salt or kosher salt. You can also use a stainless-steel scrubber or similar product. I've even used metal bristle brushes. As soon as your iron piece is clean, put it on heat to dry, and then season at once to keep the rust from returning.

This method is not quite as thorough as all-over heat, because you run the risk of missing some rust.

Chemical Stripping Oven Cleaners

In a well-ventilated outdoor area or a garage with the doors open, spray your ironware thoroughly with oven cleaning spray. Sprays that foam will work best because they will stick on the iron longer and work their chemical process quickly and usually more efficiently than the natural options. It's important to work in a well-ventilated area and use proper safety equipment when using chemical cleaners, so wear safety glasses and rubber gloves when handling these sprays. Check the manufacturer's label.

Once sprayed, wrap the iron piece in plastic (a large trash bag works great) and place it in a plastic bin large enough to hold it in a safe location away from animals and small children for 48 hours. The bin will contain any leakage from the plastic bag.

After 48 hours, open the plastic bag and check. If some of the rust or debris remains stuck to the pan, close the bag and let sit for another 24 hours. Depending on the depth of the rust and the oven cleaner used, it may take 4 days or more to eat down to the iron below.

Wash with warm water and soap (or scrub with salt and then wash), and season immediately.

Seasoning can be done to a raw cast-iron pan, a stripped pan of any age, or a seasoned cast-iron pan you're adding more seasoning layers to for upkeep or your preference. Seasoning can be done a variety of ways from these three starting places, but never attempt to season with a piece of rusty cast iron. You must remove the rust first, using the oven, fire, vinegar, or chemical-stripping processes listed above, or your seasoning work can (and likely will!) fail due to the iron oxide (rust!) sitting under the seasoning layers.

You will also need to be aware of your oiling activity. It's important to rub your preferred oil all over the pan: inside, outside, on the handles, and inside any handle holes. The curves by handles where they meet the base and inside those handle holes are easily missed but will rust fast if not coated with the rest of the piece. You'll also want to make sure not to fill any indented logos with too much oil. I find a cotton rag the best tool for any seasoning attempts, no matter what way (oven or fire) you choose to season.

Oven Seasoning

Place any clean/raw/stripped ironware, or ironware you'd like to put another coat on, upside down in a cold oven with an initial layer of oil on it. I recommend putting a sheet pan on the rack below the skillet to catch any debris or oil drippings. Set the oven temperature to 400°F. When it reaches the correct temperature, set the timer for 1 hour. (You can also season at 500°F for the first coat or two, especially if you had to strip the iron first.)

Make sure your kitchen is well ventilated—turn on big fans and kitchen fans, and open windows. The cast iron is not actually seasoning and bonding with the oil until you see smoke . . . so fans and open windows will hopefully keep the fire department away!

When the hour is up, shut off the oven but leave the pan in for another hour. Some people prefer to pull out the hot iron, season it again at once, and stick it back in the oven (it cuts your oven time in half). That is perfectly doable, but the pan is very hot and can be hard to handle in a kitchen.

In an hour's time, remove the iron from the oven and add another very thin layer of oil. Stick the iron back in the oven, reset the oven temperature to 400°F (or 500°F), and set the timer for 1 hour. When the hour is up, once again shut off the oven, but leave the pan in the oven for another hour to cool slightly.

To achieve a glossy shiny black finish, you should repeat the entire process at least five times. So . . . yeah, at least 10 hours of work!

It's a lengthy process, so find a show to binge-watch while you do this. Cast iron takes quite a bit of energy to heat fully. Not only is it slow to heat, it is slow to cool, and due to its metal/graphite molecular structure and the way it retains temperatures, it takes a while to respond to heat changes. But well-seasoned cast iron is a kitchen staple and worth the work.

Fire Seasoning

To season cast iron over a flame, prepare a wood fire as you would a typical bonfire or campfire using the appropriate safety tools and precautions. Do not use coals—they will not be hot enough. Protect yourself from getting hot-oil burns by wearing welding gloves, closed shoes, long pants, long sleeves, and eye safety glasses, plus a hat for hair!

Place a grill rack over the wood, and to keep from getting marks or lines on the iron from the rack, either set a brick on the grill to hold the ironware or plan to wedge a corner of the ironware into a slat in the grill so it is slightly suspended over the grill plate. When the fire is hot (I use an oven thermometer held 18 inches above the fire with a minimum goal temperature of 220°F—you want the temperature to be over the boiling point of water), place the ironware over the flames. Leave the ironware on the fire until the iron starts to turn bluish.

Pull the ironware off the fire, spray and rub a very thin coat of your oil or fat preference over the entire piece with a cotton rag, and place it immediately back onto the fire. You'll know that the iron is truly hot enough if this initial coat of oil smokes slightly as you apply it. If the iron gets too hot, the oil or fat will explode into flames and burn off upon contact. You'll have to start over (so know your oil's smoke point!), which is annoying.

Then . . . wait. Typically, a properly hot fire will cause the coat of oil to polymerize (dry with heat to "harden" the oil) within 5 to 15 minutes, depending on outside air temperature (Think of Wisconsin in January! It takes so long to heat up a fire!), consistency of the fire temperature, and type of oil used. You may find you can get six coats on in an hour. And don't forget to keep feeding your flames—tending your wood in the fire requires constant vigilance! (Have a lot of beer available for the friends watching from the sidelines.)

Although this is the traditional method and a bit trickier to accomplish than oven seasoning, it's more energy efficient and faster to complete.

Seasoning cast-iron skillets over an open
fire. Caveat: You cannot be afraid of fire!

THE AMERICAN SKILLET COMPANY

Alisa also lives in Wisconsin, and we spoke on the phone very early in my exploration into designing a cookware line. She was incredibly supportive, even while juggling her own growing business. We ended up meeting at one of the large housewares events in Chicago years later. Serendipity put our booths across from each other, so we had plenty of time to exchange tips, share trade gossip, and drink some beers. She has since become a wonderful resource and a solid friend. We makers like to stick together, after all.

What are the biggest difficulties with manufacturing cast-iron wares?

I think the biggest barrier to achieving high-quality cookware starts with the level of investment, both financially and energetically, that is needed to start and successfully finish the whole manufacturing process of turning a concept into a piece of cookware. Cookware has a whole different level of compliance than, say, the farm implement and auto industries. It's held to as many artistic and aesthetic standards as it is to the metallurgical and technical developments that are needed to produce an artfully crafted product that people want to touch and live with for literally generations to come.

In today's manufacturing climate, foundries are pressured to compete so aggressively on pricing and production output that many job shops are just not suitably set up to take on the demands of making quality cookware in their facility. There's a special dedication and understanding needed by the manufacturer who is willing to take on the high standards required for producing a quality piece of cookware consistently. Everyone needs to be on board with the amount of work it takes to accomplish it, and there simply is no cutting corners allowed.

What's the most exciting thing about it?

What I love the most about my role inside the manufacturing process is that there is a high level of camaraderie established with my team and business colleagues, from industrial processing to customer reviews and new retail relationships. We're making products that don't have a planned obsolescence attached to them. We are invested in long-term relationships with our customers and manufacturing partners, and our creations are meant to be meaningful heirlooms in the families and businesses that use them.

Why choose to work with cast iron over, say, aluminum or stainless steel?

My relationship to casting metal started as an art student in Milwaukee around 2001, where the typical fine-arts expectation for sculpture students would be to celebrate the use of casting aluminum and bronze for sculptural concepts.

But I had a special opportunity to be introduced to iron casting early on as a freshman, and the process combined with the utilitarian potential of the metal absolutely fascinated me. It's a metal that is found literally everywhere in our daily environment, and I really loved the familiarity of that, too. It went beyond the label of "art metal," and the industrial, decorative, and domestic attributes of cast iron intrigued me deeply. I was more interested in engaging my audience in a new way, by creating kinetic, performative, and usable objects.

What are your favorite tricks for seasoning cast iron at home?

We are a bit ruthless when it comes to cooking at home, so we have a ritual of cleaning and maintenance after every meal for which we use our cast-iron cookware. We love to caramelize onions, bake gooey s'mores, and make cheesy dips in the pans, so we have lots of practice cleaning and keeping our seasoning up to snuff.

For the sticky onions and baked-on marshmallows, our number one trick to releasing the mess is to first boil a little water in the pan to soften it up. Using a plastic scraper, get as much off as possible, then lay a generous fistful of coarse salt in the pan. Find one of those old potatoes sitting in the pantry and cut it in half to use it for scrubbing down the surface, removing any remaining gunk. [Potatoes have oxalic acid and clean up rust and oxidation well, but anything with oxalic acid will work, such as rhubarb or sweet potatoes.] I always follow up with a wee bit of soap and a quick rinse with a soft sponge, then head into my postcleaning ritual of maintenance on my seasoning.

My ritual after cleaning is:

Dry: Completely dry the skillet with a towel and place over the heat on the range top for a minute or two.

Oil: Drop a quarter-size amount of your preferred cooking oil into the dry pan. (We like flaxseed, or canola works fine, too; it's really your preference. Don't overthink it.)

Rub: Rub it *all* around, almost as if you're trying to wipe the oil completely off. Make sure to get into every nook and cranny. Do not leave any puddles or drips anywhere; the goal is to have an ultra-thin layer of oil over the whole pan.

Bake: This is the real magic. Heat the oven to at least 450°F and bake the pan for a minimum of 10 minutes if you're in a rush, or 30 to 60 minutes if it's really needing some TLC. The goal is to get it to smoke a bit, so make sure to turn on the fan or open some windows! The oil needs to polymerize from a liquid to a solid state, and each oil has its own smoke point, so just watch it.

Cool: Let the pan cool down slowly and naturally and store it wherever you keep your cookware.

Cleaning your cast iron properly will provide longevity to the seasoning you've put down. You don't need to be precious about it, and it's not hard to do once you get used to it. Frequently used cast iron needs less intensive care after each use than those pieces you pull out occasionally, but you'll want to treat your seasoning well by taking care of it so it treats your food nicely in return!

Quick Cleaning Method

I recommend you only clean this fast way if you plan to use the cast-iron piece again within 2 to 3 weeks, because it's a little "hackish." That said, it's great for parents on the go or if you know you'll be pulling the ironware out sooner than the next holiday cook-off. It's not necessary to do every time if you have a well-seasoned piece, but it's a great way to help add another layer of seasoning for a newly seasoned or brand-new cast-iron ware.

1. Wash the ironware in warm water and use a soft brush or rag to remove any debris that won't come off with your hands. A small amount of nonabrasive soap or salt can help if you so wish.

2. Dry thoroughly and quickly with a cloth.

3. While the iron is still warm, place a small amount of the oil of your choice on the iron and rub a fine coating across the entire piece. A soft cotton towel or a piece of paper towel works great for this.

4. Put the pan away or hang it on a rack.

5. The next time you use the piece, heat it quite high so the oil polymerizes (bakes on) before adding food. You should always heat the cast iron before adding food anyway, but leave it on the heat for several minutes longer if you have a fresh coat of oil on it.

Thorough Cleaning Method

For an iron piece that won't get much use for a while (we're talking months or years), you'll want to ensure that no water has snuck around any weakly seasoned points, or the next time you pull out the iron you might see some early or superficial rust spots starting to oxidize. For you zealous cast-iron aficionados, collectors, or those who simply like to be completely thorough, I recommend the following process for cleaning:

1. Wash the ironware in warm water and use a soft brush or rag to remove any debris that won't come off with your hands. A bit of small, nonabrasive soap can also be used in a tiny amount or salt if you so wish.

2. Dry thoroughly and quickly with a cloth.

3. Place in the oven or on the stovetop over medium heat and heat to 250°F to burn off any microscopic water still sitting on the iron. Water boils at 212°F, so you'll be safe at 250°F.

4. Using oven mitts, pull the iron piece off the heat. Carefully apply a small amount of the oil of your choice and rub a fine coating on the entire piece. A soft cotton towel or a piece of paper towel works great for this.

5. Put the piece back in the oven or on the stove, crank the heat up to 400°F on an oven or high heat on the stove, and bake the coat of oil into your seasoning for at least 1 hour.

6. Let cool before putting away.

Great Products

I have two go-to tools for cleaning my cast iron, and I use them both for everyday cleaning and when I'm preparing to put a piece into storage. I love that cast iron is so easy to clean or store if it's seasoned well!

1. Pampered Chef nylon pan scrapers

2. Briwax paste wax with beeswax

That Buttery Super-Smooth Iron

So many people covet that silky-smooth patina you find in cast iron that has been lovingly cared for, seasoned, and cleaned properly over the centuries. Collectors and cooks alike rave about the satin finish of vintage pieces from defunct Griswold and Wagner brands.

The shiny smoothness does not actually do a single thing in terms of the cast iron's performance. It will still heat slowly (and slightly unevenly) until it reaches its full (even) potential over your flame. That's the nature of iron, period. But those old pieces sure are gorgeous (and some people have been working hard to replicate those smooth surfaces once again, with drool-worthy results).

Smooth cast iron is purely an aesthetic preference. Some people prefer an uneven surface because they believe the porosity and small bumps help the iron "hold on to" the seasoning better. Again, it's all about personal preference and belief! Cast iron is good for keeping the dialogue alive.

Those smooth vintage pans were fine sand casted—meaning the molds used were packed with an exceptionally fine grain sand. They also were often milled or polished (different processes but with relatively similar results), meaning the ironware was ground against a wheel to create a smooth interior. This is a labor-intensive process and renders the cast-iron pieces even pricier. Finally, some of those vintage, smooth iron pieces have almost two hundred years of wear and tear. I wonder what they looked like brand new off the foundry floor!

If your pan is seasoned properly, it will be nonstick no matter the type of finish.

Personally, I have a few vintage pieces and a few modern ones. Why? Because it's fun to have some slippery, soft skillets as well as some locally made rough-and-tumble ones—they all work the same, and variety is the spice of life!

There are a handful of widely accepted rules when it comes to cast-iron care. They're easy to remember and are similar to the dos and don'ts that come with copper cookware.

⇒DO⇐

1. Wipe out excess food and oils and leave the pan lightly coated with any fats like bacon grease or any cooking oil for the next use (within 2 weeks).

2. Use salt to help scrub off dirt, grime, food, and superficial rust.

3. Use warm water, a soft cloth, and nonabrasive soap (a little, if desired) to wash.

4. Dry well after washing.

5. Add a little oil of your choice to the whole iron piece after it's thoroughly dried to help along the seasoning process.

6. Always heat the ironware before putting in new food to help the newest coat bake/polymerize into the iron.

⇒DON'T⇐

1. Place cast iron in the dishwasher.

2. Use sharp or metal instruments on seasoned cast iron, as they can scratch and strip off the seasoning.

3. Use metal scrubbies or abrasive cleaners for regular cleaning—they'll strip off all that hard-won seasoning.

4. Leave cast-iron pieces to sit with standing water to "soak off the food." Iron is super porous even when seasoned. You'll end up with water deep inside your ironware, and that's bad! Also, it strips off your seasoning.

INTERVIEW WITH HENRY LODGE, FOURTH-GENERATION MEMBER OF
THE LODGE CAST-IRON FAMILY

Henry Lodge holding one of the new vintage-inspired Lodge pieces, the fluted cake pan

Can you offer some history about Lodge?

Lodge was founded in 1896 by Joseph Lodge, my great-grandfather. He left his home in Pennsylvania and ended up in South Pittsburg, Tennessee. He worked at the local blast furnace, which smelted iron from the ore in the mountains, and then started his own foundry. Originally, it was named the Blacklock Foundry after the local Episcopal priest. He renamed the foundry Lodge in 1910.

What's some little-known Lodge family history?

Joe Lodge (my great-grandfather) had a son and a daughter. The daughter, Edith, married Charles Richard Kellermann and had seven children. The son, Richard Leslie Lodge, was my grandfather and had a son—my father, John Richard Lodge—as well as a daughter. I was the second of four children (I have an older brother, a younger sister, and a baby brother) and married Donna Cook. We have three children ourselves.

How did you get started in the making of heirloom cast iron?

My father, John Richard Lodge, was born and raised in South Pittsburg. He became an Episcopal priest, so I grew up moving every four years or so. I remember visiting my grandparents but didn't know much about the family business until I entered college at Sewanee, just twenty-five miles from South Pittsburg. I began working at Lodge during the summer I graduated from the university in 1972. The rest, as they say, is history.

What's your favorite piece of Lodge cast iron?

Probably the fluted cake pan. That pan will make a beautiful cake with a nice crust. One of my college professors would occasionally treat some of his psychology majors to a delicious orange cake with a Grand Marnier glaze. He passed that recipe on to my wife when we got married. My go-to skillet at home, on the other hand, is our 10-inch chef skillet. It's the perfect size for the two of us whether we're making spaghetti sauce or eggs or searing steak.

What do you believe is important about manufacturing cookware?

It is a wonderful legacy my great-grandfather, Joseph Lodge, left for his family and all the folks who are a part of the Lodge Manufacturing Company. It's exciting to know that we manufacture a product that is inexpensive, will prepare delicious food, and will last a lifetime. I am passionate about our company and our cast iron, because together, they provide four hundred team members in southeast Tennessee with the means to enjoy life and provide for their families. That is a one-hundred-and-twenty-three-year-old (and counting!) winning proposition. Thank you, Joseph Lodge!

A big Lodge cast-iron Dutch oven. I use this for baking pies in fires at reenactments.

The biggest change in making cast iron over the past hundred years has come about because the Industrial Revolution buoyed all industry. Without cast iron, though, that particular revolution would have not been the same: no cast-iron to make machine parts, which in turn made more products and items, which made them less expensive for regular folks, which eventually created a new social class.

Foundries have replaced forges and blast furnaces to create cast iron using huge processing machines and giant vats for charges (the melting/mixing furnace pot of molten iron). Some larger foundries have been able to mechanize almost the entire creation of ironware, including the seasoning. Smaller foundries may combine hand-pouring with a processing machine or two, and still tinier boutique companies may individually create and custom design each piece. There's no right or wrong way to build cast-iron cookware, and one of the beauties of cast iron is its affordability and longevity.

Beyond the mechanics of actually making cast iron, though, is our nostalgia. Even though it's historically inaccurate, we all have these pioneer visions of cowboys out on the prairie with their horses, cooking a bit of supper over a small fire in their handy cast-iron skillet. Ironically, most cowboys didn't travel with individual cast-iron pieces; the weight would have been too much for the horses. Cowboys without a mess wagon near would have used tinware. We think of immigrant mothers wielding giant portions in even bigger black pots. Some of us might have family recipes cooked in cast iron. And there's something deep and heart pulling about visions like that.

But when I think of cast iron, I think of fire: the extreme fire needed in the furnace to melt the iron and the way the metal itself looks like bright lava when it's poured into molds to create cookware. Fire is needed to season ironware and make the surface a pure, satin-like black. And the pans sit over or in fire to make meals and have done so for hundreds of years.

So every time you hold a piece of ironware in your hands, know you're touching a technology and a deep recognition of a widely used metal embedded in our collective world history. That's certainly something to get fired up about!

A stack of my House Copper skillets, freshly seasoned with organic kosher North Dakota flaxseed oil (how's that for a mouthful?!)

CLAY

I'm absolutely, totally horrific at making anything out of clay. I'm apparently able to swirl molten tin around over a fire, and I have the arm strength for hammering on metal. Give me a paintbrush, watercolors, acrylics, or even pastels, and I'm good. But put me in front of a pottery wheel? It's a crap show! I press too hard or not enough, and everything always wobbles. But clay in cookware unites all world cultures, so here's a chunk of history, science, use, and care of all things made of earth!

In high school, I loved art class with such a passion that I think it frightened my father, who kept telling me that art was a hobby, not a career. He said such things out of love and the desire to keep me from being a starving artist (jury is still out if my cookware qualifies me as one). Had the only unit in art class been pottery, I would have definitely agreed with him.

I can still remember Mrs. Beranek, the long-term art teacher, pulling out the wheels and gathering us around.

"We'll be working with clay for a few weeks," she announced.

I felt my stomach plummet as I glanced longingly back at the acrylics and watercolors on the tables. *Damn! I'm gonna suck at this.* I already had a sense of my potential from previous middle-school attempts, but I still nurtured some hope that my hands might figure it out.

No such luck. I think Mrs. Beranek might have been a little shocked at my lack of talent, because I was so clearly uncoordinated at the potter's wheel.

I gave up and started to work with clay on the table, avoiding the wheel. Mrs. Beranek came by and stopped.

"What are you making?" she asked.

I glanced at the lumpy pieces on the table. "Sculpture."

"Ah. Of what?"

"I think maybe like . . . Aphrodite rising from the sea?"

She looked doubtful. "Keep it appropriate, Sara."

"What do you mean?"

"No nudity."

I looked back at the clumpy gray material and flexed my fingers, where the clay dried and itched under my nails and made my skin feel thick and cumbersome for hours after washing. I hadn't thought about keeping it PG rated, but I suppose she was right.

Well, Aphrodite saved me, because I didn't fail that unit of art class, though it would be extremely generous to call that little "statue" sculpture.

In college, one of my friends said we should take a pottery class at a studio in downtown Milwaukee. Once again I was doubtful, but hey—there's always hope! The studio was run by a man about ten years older than us who had a gigantic original painting by Warhol or Picasso or someone famous on his wall (some artist I turned out to be!). He had developed a gorgeous glaze that looked like exploding blue blooms across the surface of the clay after firing.

Turns out I was still not very good at pottery. But at least in college we could drink wine after failed tries at making pretty or useful (I'd take either) pottery.

My mother graciously kept my dilapidated attempts, either from parental affection or to save my feelings. Every once in a while, she still brings one over to my house, saying she's "cleaning out the basement" and thought I might like my old art. Hmmm . . .

So while the skill of pottery making has eluded me and likely will continue to do so, it's an art form I respect tremendously in the hands of others. Potters create gorgeous sculpture, beautiful designs, and practical, usable vessels. They're carrying on a tradition stretching back ten thousand years while putting their own definitive mark on each piece they make. Like the copper cookware from my garage shop, their work will also likely be found in an archaeological dig thousands of years from now. That connection to both the past and the future is tremendously cool as well as deeply human and full of heart. We've been using clay cookware for thousands of years and will be for a long time yet. It's probably the most timeless of all cookware and deserves a love affair of its own.

Up to this point, I've waxed on about metal—iron, tin, and copper. Clay is different. First, it isn't an element unto itself; you won't find it in the periodic table as you will tin, copper, and iron. Clay is made from the earth, and hundreds of different elements and molecules are part of its chemical makeup. This means it's more variable and less controllable, though we've learned how to measure and mix different kinds and proportions of clay, sediment, rock, and dirt to make more reliable firings.

Unlike metals, clay didn't start out being used in warfare. Clay was first primarily used to create statues and forms for worship purposes; then it found more practical application in the kitchen. Using clay is an extension of heartfelt sincerity: the providing of love and care for fellow human beings, whether for sustenance or faith. I'm not a romantic person by nature, but I do recognize the thread of love and romance that binds us to our history, past, food, and one another.

I find it fascinating how clay's history and impact on the world differ from that of metals. Clay allowed people to boil water longer, without fear that the heat would burn through an animal hide set over the flames. We could make food and save it for later in clay vessels. We could use it to store the finds from hunts or berry pickings. As we learned to ferment bever-

Creating the pottery pieces in my head was the easy part. The reality required a potter's touch.

ages, we could keep beer and wine cool and away from the sun's rays. (See, I can bring any discussion back to booze. It's a talent.)

Even though there was no way my own skills (or lack thereof) would allow me to add making bowls and crockery to my endless to-do list, I knew I wanted clay pieces in my cookware line. When I undertook the task of sourcing and purchasing pottery items to help create my version of the American kitchen, I began by looking for experts. Pottery designs are not as straightforward as those of cast-iron skillets or copper pots. Different glazes, sizes, styles, decorations, and colors have been used over centuries. There are different grades of clay, from soft varieties to porcelain. I already knew that porcelain was outside my scope: Although it was developed in China more than fifteen hundred years ago, it was not part of the American kitchen as made by local potters. So I narrowed down my search to more basic clay products for the cookware line and left the fancy porcelain to others.

When I looked for designs online, in books, and in antiques stores that fit my vision of traditional pottery that might have been used by the pioneers whose copper and iron pieces I'd built my line on, I couldn't always easily tell if they were traditional American creations or something brought over from Europe by an immigrant. While many of the designs in antiques stores came from around the world and became "Americanized" over time, I wanted something simple that reminded one of an early sod-house or western kitchen, something perhaps made by a local artisan. Simple and clean. Spongeware—which looks exactly like it sounds, with the pottery blotted with glaze that looks like a sponge job with paint—was popular during the pioneer years, but frankly I didn't think it would sell very well. I mean, the design can become garish very easily.

In the end, I settled on a solid, simple design: a plain, soft, ivory clay, with a bit of blue around the rim, like the line of a horizon or the ocean. Even if it was a bit prettier than some pottery found on traditional American hearths in the 1800s, the design felt like a classic, and that was important, too.

So much of our kitchen pottery today isn't really what it was like in the old days. Not only is it manufactured by machine overseas, where one doesn't know the chemical makeup of the clay or the glazes, but the walls are thin and the quality of the baked earth is weak. Why else do handles break off easily and bottoms and rims chip at the first use? Traditional pottery was made by hand, had thick walls intended to resist wear and tear, and was covered in glazes made from local sources. So whether you'd call it a bowl "like Grandma used" or a vintage reproduction, I wanted something that would one day be listed in an estate sale as an antique in excellent condition, with decades of use to come.

But no way was I going to build a pottery studio in my garage; I needed some professional help! Like other parts of my journey to make a cookware line, it started off a bit bumpy. I began with a lot of cold calls (again) and spoke to a number of potters. Most worked alone, so when I called about discussing custom pieces, they thought I meant a single one.

"No," I explained. "I want to create vintage-looking wares, have them made by hand, and order like thirty of each at once."

"Oooh, really?" Typically there was a long pause on the other end of the line. "Like volume?"

"Yeah."

"I don't really do volume. It's too hard for a single person. Or, if I did, it would be so expensive you couldn't sell it for reasonable retail."

I'd hang up and think, *I don't care how many people I have to call, there is no way I'm doing this part!*

In the beginning, I finally found a single artist who decided to tackle it. It took her a while, and she ended up feeling overwhelmed by the order. "It's too much to do," she explained. "I'm so sorry, and I love clay, but doing all the pieces instead of one or two artistic ones is just not what I can do."

Back to the drawing board I went! I so love the internet, though, because once I started looking again, I hit upon the woman-owned and -operated Rowe Pottery in Wisconsin, which employs a few master potters full-time. Of course, I had to make sure the bowls would be made of pure clay both sourced and mixed locally (made in the USA is a big deal to me). It was important that each piece be slightly different and dried naturally (without artificial "help"), so that it would react to its environment better when used for cooking and baking. For visual appeal, I wanted each piece to have the gentle, soft look of hand-painted pottery.

Now, I had to pay for them. Even though I planned to have a very tiny amount in stock, I won't kid you—it can be expensive to have each piece created by hand. Sometimes it is double what it would cost if I had the wares made overseas or by slip-casting (see page 178) here in the USA.

Discovering Rowe Pottery in Cambridge, Wisconsin, and their master potters

Yikes! But it has been well worth it, and the work supports several small, local companies and artisans. I also received the extra gift of friendship and personal collaboration with incredibly skilled artists, all giving a little love to keeping a ten-thousand-year-old trade alive. Priceless.

Pottery is incredibly familiar and intimate but also remains a bit of an enigma. It comes in myriad shapes and sizes, colors, and styles, and in completely different cultural designs. And yet in the end, it's the thing that draws all our cultures together. It was the first cooking pot for all of us.

Before metal, we had only clay, an earthy material (pun intended) that was the fabric of our cookware. Ancient pottery reached beyond borders, meshed cultures, and created a road map that archaeologists use to document history: trends, traveling paths, and time periods. It was the original substance from which pots, bowls, and cauldrons were made and is by far the most ancient cookware, preceded only by roughly hollowed pieces of stone, bone, and wood. As the ancestor of kitchen tools, it deserves a solid retelling of its history, so we can properly appreciate the current pottery and ceramics gracing our kitchen counters today.

Even before the Stone Age, ceramics were used by many cultures across the globe. The first use of fired clay was for religious ceremonies (in contrast, copper and iron were first used for war). The firing of earth to create something new must have seemed magical, a theme that is explored to strong effect in the novels of Jean M. Auel. Sometimes it would not harden and would fall apart in soft lumps. Other times, it would shatter or explode. Our ancestors' efforts were trial and error as they slowly and painstakingly discovered the ways earth and clay could be mastered.

The oldest known clay piece is a female-shaped figurine dating back nearly twenty-nine thousand years—give or take a millennium or two. It was fired at a low temperature. This is the Venus of Dolní Věstonice, which is slightly older and less famous than the Venus of Willendorf. Both Venuses are small in size and were likely carried all over by their nomadic makers. No matter where they were from, our early ancestors did not live in cities or stable cultural communities. Rather, they followed the seasons and their prey as other beasts did. Only tools, language, and some artistic endeavors, like the clay figurines, separated us from other animals. Large, heavy "domestic" wares were cumbersome; our ancestors' way of life did not support bulky, breakable items to be lugged along over the vast fields and forests of the ancient world. It made sense that the first shapers and artists of clay would instead replicate objects that already existed in horn and bone: human or animal figures. This type of ceramic creation has been discovered in many locations, from the fields of ancient Moravia to the islands of Japan.

The oldest ceramic pots found in the Xianrendong Cave of the Jiangxi Province in southeast China—dated between eighteen thousand and twenty thousand years old—show how the Eastern civilizations surpassed the West in creating clay pots that were not only functional but decorative, signifying a calmness and settling of their culture. The people of the Jōmon culture in Japan (ca. 10,500 BCE) were already making both figurines and cookware from clay as well. Like their Chinese neighbors across the water, the Jōmon were advanced in terms of working clay to create both pretty *and* useful items. They mixed the clay with organic material, such as fibers, crushed seashells, and possibly glittery, thin rock formations like mica or lead, to help adhere the layers together. Jōmon pots are typically deep containers with pointy bottoms.

Meanwhile, the oldest settled Neolithic society discovered in the West and what is now Europe is considered to be Catal Huyuk (Çatalhöyük) on the Anatolian peninsula (modern-day Turkey), dating back nearly sixty-five hundred years. Lovely clay pots have been discovered there, signifying a stabilization of Neolithic culture in the West.

Agriculture first developed in the Fertile Crescent in today's Middle East, and it flowed into the surrounding areas relatively quickly. This swath of land, sometimes called the cradle of civilization, gave birth to villages as people domesticated animals and planted grains, ending their nomadic way of life. We have the revolution of farming to thank for creating a desire for more permanent cookware, especially once the development of low-heat "furnaces" led to efficient firing of clay, and people weren't dependent only on campfires and buried fires for making their wares.

Why is firing so necessary? Before it's fired, the clay is filled with water and acts accordingly—the earth will dry out or turn muddy, depending on the weather or the humidity. Unfortunately, there are no written records available, so archaeologists can only hypothesize about when the proper temperature and timing for firing clay was discovered based on their finds. (This is a splendid example of a scientific wild-assed guess.)

Rooms with a view (of pottery!)
at Rowe Pottery in historic
Cambridge, Wisconsin

The Three Types of Ceramics

NAME	CHARACTERISTICS
Earthenware: the first and oldest type of pottery, created in the Paleolithic, Mesolithic, and Neolithic periods	Soft and slightly dense, the clay was generally fired between 1,832°F and 2,192°F. Earthenware was usually made of local clay, the exception being the elite and nobility, who had access to porcelain and metal cookware as time passed. Cord decorated, slab method, and coiled pottery (see page 174) are (ancient) examples of earthenware. Most pottery found in archaeological digs is earthenware, though in China some very early stoneware may be found.
Stoneware: the most common type of pottery made from the 1300s onward .	Dense, fired only once in a kiln between 2,012°F and 2,372°F, early stoneware was popular in Western culture after the fourteenth century, when the Renaissance swept the continent and the information about making stoneware reached the West from the East. Because of the additional hardness stoneware offers, it swiftly became the preference of pottery makers once their kilns caught up to the technology. Stoneware is still in use today.
Porcelain: a white, translucent pottery invented in China in the 600s	Fine, thin walled, and more perishable due to its easy breakability, porcelain is fired at a temperature higher than 2,552°F and is put in the kiln twice. Porcelain is made of clay, flint, and silica and was often "faked" in the early years by those who wanted to make a lot of money! It is still considered formal, expensive, and special to this day.

After forming, all pottery needs to be dried and fired. The earliest ovens for pottery baking were simply the same ground fires used for roasting meats; dried clay pieces were buried in the coals. Even when firing clay moved beyond its experimental phase, scholars believe that most kilns still consisted of a hole in the dirt over which a huge bonfire was lit. A bonfire would likely not provide constant flames of over 1,000°F, the minimum amount of heat needed to make earthenware, the softest type of pottery. You'd want that steady 1,000°F heat for hours and hours to ensure your design didn't fall apart, and ideally you'd hit the 1,200°F mark at times.

Think about any fire you've built. It takes a long time to get to those perfect coals at the base, and the temperature there is still pretty variable. Now consider fires back in the day: Even if they were made and buried underground, heat could easily escape from any holes or be absorbed by the earth. Without a steady temperature, pottery won't heat up properly, so it's probable that early clay pieces failed a lot.

The firing of clay figurines and vessels would have increasingly improved as communities discovered the benefits of solid, watertight cookware. By 10,000 BCE, groups of Neolithic people were settling into farming practices. Once people were no longer nomadic, heavy, more permanent clay cooking pots and storage containers became more appealing and grew to be a part of the overarching culture.

This was a gigantic technological leap. Suddenly we had new jobs! A better way to cook! Earthenware kitchen equipment became a hot commodity as has been shown over and over by archaeological digs. (Seriously, check out *Archaeology* magazine! No, its reps aren't paying me to say so. It's just fascinating!) Pottery pieces have been found at thousand of historic dig sites, from Africa, Iceland, and Japan to hidden cities in the jungles of South America. Archaeological digs can be dated based on the age and style of the pottery found there. Each clay shard reveals a story with its thickness, composition, and decorative style. Pottery is history's atlas.

CLAY TECHNOLOGY

The first clay cookware in the West was most likely of the "pinch pot" variety (not much different from those pinch pots your children might bring home from school), which would have been a quick and easy design shift after pushing and pressing clay into human shapes. But soon new ways of creating clay cookware were developed. Western and Eastern potters alike formed pottery exclusively by hand. The typical method started with a flat base of circular clay. They'd build up the pot by coiling a rope of clay vertically around the base, then press or smooth down the coils using pressure from either the potter's hand or tools (as in the case of the Jōmon potters).

After the coiling process, the next preferred method of clay cookware production was the slab method, in which the clay was flattened and pieced together. Flattening had the benefit of removing air bubbles, so firing did not result in as many explosions or ruined wares. The slab method was used in making bricks for buildings and creating different structures for cookware vessels and likely led to the development of specific clay tools for shaping and cutting. Most Neolithic pottery found today is undecorated. On those pieces that do have markings, they were cut or pressed into the clay before firing.

By about 7000 BCE, ancient Egyptians had created glazes, and a new art form took over the world. Suddenly it was possible to create vessels that reflected the design preferences of the current culture. When we find vases that outline ancient sexual practices or funeral rites, that's all thanks to the invention of pottery glaze. Without the invention of glazes, pottery might have fallen largely out of use with the advent of metal crafts. But glazes allowed pottery to be longer lasting, less porous or leaky, durable enough to handle daily wear and tear, and most importantly, visually appealing.

After the development of earthenware, there was little change in pottery's physical makeup until kilns were invented as a means to fire pottery in groups at hot enough temperatures. The first kilns likely sprouted in what is now Iraq around 6000 BCE. Initially, they were only "pit" kilns: large pits dug and lined with materials that would burn easily, such as wood and leaves. These quickly gave way to stone-lined kilns that allowed for higher and more stable temperatures. That stabilization of heat further allowed for more durable pots and eventually paved the way for stoneware to be formed and fired.

Pottery drying on racks before
entering the kiln for firing

Somewhere between 6000 and 4000 BCE, the potter's wheel was invented in Mesopotamia. This was a major breakthrough in technology, because now one went from sitting on the ground and building up a piece of clay to sitting on a chair and using a simple machine to expedite the creation of pottery, especially any piece with a hollow center. Early potter's wheels were large, likely made of wood, and used to slowly rotate coils of clay, which sped up the hand-coiling process. Then around 4000 BCE, Chalcolithic metalsmithing, such as smelting, took off, which led to new advancements in the creation of ovens or furnaces that could bake at higher, longer-lasting, and more even temperatures, resulting in better firing. Kilns became more efficient and could be fired as high as 2,192°F. Wheels became faster, too, using the "flywheel" balance, which harnessed the kinetic energy of the stone wheel, pushed by apprentices or by the potter's foot. These advances created products that we'd easily recognize as true stoneware.

The next several thousand years saw changes in the designs and dimensions of pottery vessels, glazes, and decorations. Although technology had created cheaper iron pots so more people could afford metal cookware, clay remained the primary choice for storing and cooking food. Our ancestors continued to rely on such a dependable and versatile tool, which had been around tens of thousands of years. Into the Middle Ages, earthenware used for cooking, cleaning, bathing, and holding fat for a wick graced the hearths of most people. Pottery was the material of choice for chamber pots, drinking cups, and servingware, as it was the most readily available and hard to destroy. Wine and oil kept well within the dark ceramic walls of pottery, without spoiling or going rancid as easily. Pottery could also be used over or inside a fire, and because it had been made for thousands of years, it virtually came with its own warranty. People knew it would work now and last for a long time.

Pottery was a well-known and time-honored trade around the world, and the abundance of potters meant that clay wares were accessible to nearly everyone—brand new if you could afford it or as castoffs that could be reused for generations. Even the poorest family would have been able to find a pot to cook in.

A pottery wheel in action

THE MORE THINGS CHANGE

As the Middle Ages progressed, people began to look for stout, sturdy ironware, not realizing the clay jars they discarded for a more "durable" iron pot would in fact long outlast the black metal, which has potential for rust. Archaeologists struggle to find whole pieces of ironware from digs that date from, say, 1100 CE, but we find pottery shards thousands of years older.

What does this mean? Pottery has never left our kitchens! It's like our own living fossil! We still use it to bake pies and store oil, but its presence is taken for granted, and it underwent a gigantic change in terms of importance by the mid-1700s, when metal became an affordable and common kitchenware material. At this point, pottery was relegated for preserving and storing, mixing and baking, instead of for cooking itself. Cooks used it for whipping up batters and baking pies, but it generally no longer held soups and meats in the way that it did for millennia before.

That is until recently, when the merits of using organic materials became important again, and we've all started to ask about where our goods are made and who made them—which brings us full circle back to the original makers of the first cookware: the clay pot. You can't go wrong with thousands and thousands of years of knowledge.

HANDMADE VS. SLIP-CASTING VS. MACHINE-MADE POTTERY

Today, most clay cookware is made by machine in large factories outside the United States. These products are relatively inexpensive and widely available, but they are typically made of lower-quality raw materials and can easily chip and break. In America, the biggest creators of pottery manufacture stoneware using a slip-casting method, which is a molding/fabricating technique that provides a sturdy product. Finally, there's the time-honored method using the wheel and hand tools, which can be customized. These handmade pieces are usually quite strong because the walls of the products are generally thicker.

So what's the difference?

Machine Made

Clay arrives at factories in powder form, which is mixed with water using huge mechanical spatulas and paddles to create *slurry.* The slurry is filter pressed to remove excess water. Now called *cake,* the clay is milled and butchered to cut out any air bubbles and formed into bricks or cylinders for the jiggering machine. This machine feeds the material into preprogramed plaster molds and can make up to nine pieces of *greenware* (prefered pottery) per minute. Another machine heats the pieces, removes any rough edges, and puts the pieces on a belt for more drying. The entire process is efficient and makes for lots of accessible and inexpensive clay wares for the home.

Slip-Casting

Slip-casting is also machinery driven, but it allows for more delicate work as well as sturdier products. The slurry is still placed into a plaster mold, but it's allowed to dry on its own. What I personally love about this pro-

Decorating pottery before firing

cess is it's a little more old school than the forced drying in machine-made wares. When the piece is dry enough, the mold is split open and the rough edges and seams are removed. The final drying is done by machine. So, while slip-casting is still considered a machine-led process, it also has a lot more touchy-feely elements from human hands.

Handmade

Handmade pottery can be either completely hand formed or spun on a wheel with hand pressure used to create the form. (I've taken dozens of pottery classes, and whatever method I've tried, my finished products are . . . suboptimal.) Items crafted by hand are art, but as beautiful as they are, they also have the thickest and sturdiest walls. Most small potters have

The cream-colored bowl and jug are hand-spun on a wheel,
whereas the dark brown bottle is slip-cast.

their clay sourced locally or from around the United States and then mixed
to their particular specifications. For instance, one might source ball clay,
which is mined in Tennessee, because it is known for adding plasticity to
ceramics. Or perhaps a potter wants the red clay found in Ohio, used in
earthenware for an intense red color after firing. Once a piece of handmade
pottery is formed, it is left to dry according to the weather, placed into a
kiln, glazed, painted, and fired again.

How can you tell that a piece of pottery you're purchasing is truly handmade? First, a potter will typically leave or stamp a mark into the bottom
of the piece. You'll notice that the paint or glaze appears obviously artistic.
And you might even detect some imperfections in the piece. If so, congrats!
You now have a handmade, one-of-a-kind piece to bake with or display!

I know Rebekah because she was the first potter to say "Yes!" to my idea of creating cookware in the fashion of the old pioneer kitchens. Her one-woman company, Shanel Pottery, is based in the sunlit basement of her home in West Bend, Wisconsin, only a few miles from my house. Her pieces are a mix of everything clay; some are pure art and some wares are functional. She'll paint lovely designs on tall white wares and leave some solid mugs rustic, rugged, and rough. It's a passion for her but not her day job, so eventually the volume I needed grew to be too much for her. Even though she no longer turns pieces for me, I will never forget her support and enthusiasm to try to re-create the American hearth. We still keep in touch, and it is a thrill to watch her business grow just like mine does—one piece of pottery (or copper, in my case) at a time.

How do you select the types of clay and glazes you use?

My clay and glazes are selected based on the aesthetic I'm going for with that particular piece. I get a lot of inspiration from old German stoneware pots with simple brushwork, emotion-filled human figure sculptures, and ancient ceremonial vessels. My favorites are the ones with handles and spouts with human faces or animals. I love the study of past vessel function and often contemplate how it could be used today, such as long handles for dipping a vessel into a well (which we don't have much need for these days).

What does creating with clay do for you? What do you love about it?

The thing I love about working with clay is that in order to center the clay, pull up a wall, and create a form, I need to be centered as well. It's a very calming and meditative practice. When the clay spins in my hands, my mind will wander off to ideas, memories, conversations, and sometimes no thoughts at all (when I'm lucky). I do some of my best thinking (and nonthinking) in the studio. It's very much like a self-guided therapy.

The thing I love most about handmade studio pottery is the connection with the maker that you get when using the piece. Think about holding a bowl made over a thousand years ago and what the maker was communicating with that piece. Why they made the decision to use a handle here or why they chose the particular symbol there. So many things can be learned about a person or their intention when using their work. Once you start to use handmade pieces, you can really enjoy food or drink in a whole new way. You won't want to go back to mass-produced factory slipware.

How does the firing process make cookware waterproof?

When a piece is fired properly, the clay becomes vitrified (in simple terms, glass-like), so it cannot absorb water. When clay has more "grog" (raw material containing elements like silica and alumina to help the clay retain shape on the potter's wheel), it can resist thermal shock better. Always avoid going from extreme hot to cold or cold to hot, such as placing a cold stoneware dish in a hot oven or filling a hot dish with cold water. The thermal shock of changing temperatures will cause the clay to get tiny cracks within it, which will weaken it and eventually make it much more fragile and likely to shatter, even if it doesn't break immediately.

What is the most difficult type of pottery shape to make, and why?

The most difficult shape to create for a pot is a horizontal line, such as a wide rim on a platter or a wide vase with a small foot. If the angles are not balanced properly, the weight will cause it to collapse.

"Ceramics" changed in the kitchen tremendously in the 1960s, when using Teflon as a nonstick coating on kitchen tools hit the markets hard. After the war, DuPont, the maker of polytetrafluoroethylene (PTFE), patented the slippery substance, called it Teflon, and created new, modern types of cookware with "cheap and unusable" aluminum. It helped that aluminum and PTFE easily bond together. Today, nearly all types of ceramic and aluminum cookware no longer contain Teflon, though other, newer, and untested technology has taken its place. Teflon and other similar nonstick coatings truly left marks on history. While PTFE is classified by some research companies as being potentially harmful to humans, no one has done any research to deeply test how our bodies react.

But it really comes down to performance. Do we know the true speed of coated pans? The conductivity? The heat transfer and energy efficiency? What are the ingredients in your nonstick coating? If you can't name them and pronounce them, maybe think about that a little more. If it's ceramic, question why you'd want to cook on an insulator rather than a conductor of heat. Clay should be used properly to work properly. Respect for the oldest cooking material in the world means using it not as a "healthy nonstick coating" but as it truly is: real cookware that bakes goodies and casseroles to perfection.

Bev, like me when I learned to make copper pieces, decided to try something she knew very little about, because it just felt right. Bev knew nothing about pottery when she bought the traditional Rowe Pottery and Ironworks, located in Cambridge, Wisconsin—a town with a long history of art and pottery making in particular. The business now occupies a huge historic 1920s building she's refurbished, with high walls and giant windows and a state-of-the-art kiln in back. I remember on my last visit, I marveled at the soaring ceiling and the huge vats of sloppy gray-brown clay ready for another round of mixing. Bev was jumpy that particular day; it was the first time she and her potters were trying out the new kiln. It worked beautifully, unsurprisingly.

On the walls of the shop hang tools with dried bits of old projects on the handles. The painter sits on a stool surrounded by natural light and hand-applies every design one by one. It is both a modern shop and one entirely devoted to practicing an age-old talent.

Rowe Pottery was struggling when Bev bought it, but she has turned it into a thriving business, a skill I deeply admire. And I love that I need to drive only an hour to go pick up pieces for my cookware line!

What makes pottery so special to you, and why did you choose this career and material?

When I got into the business, I knew nothing about pottery; I'd only collected it. My background was sales and marketing for a Fortune 500 company. As my family grew, I wanted my life to slow down. I wanted to enjoy time with my kids while still pursuing my career. I had been "crafty" my whole life, so when an opportunity came up to work in marketing at Rowe Pottery, I jumped at it. It was very different, going from a corporate structure with strict deadlines to an artisan culture, but it taught me to appreciate the creative process. I love how people can create things in pottery; it's amazing to me that a potter can grab a five-pound lump of clay and within minutes turn it into a functional product. I am certainly not an artist, but I love using my creativity along with our artists' talents to create new items.

The best part? Each piece is different, nothing is precise, and there's beauty in that.

How do you see the role of pottery changing from past to present?

Every year we research historical pottery forms and uses and replicate them using traditional pottery methods, from hand-throwing to hand-trimming. Pottery used to be used for storage and cooking in every single home, for everything. So a canister piece would be for meat, flour, or sugar, or people might fill their jug with whiskey. Think about it—a home wouldn't have Tupperware or even glass. We did a historical piece of pottery a few years ago that would have typically been used for meat, for example. In the 1800s, you would have layered meat and salt over and over so it wouldn't go bad over the winter, with a brine that would be created and sealed with wax to keep in moisture but prevent contamination. But a piece like that today can store flour and sugar without issue, so it's still completely relevant.

People have moved toward plastic and convenience, but it actually doesn't work as well. Pottery is going to store things better and keep them fresher.

So you use pottery in your kitchen for storage just like in the old days?
To back up, when pottery was used as a main kitchen storage vessel, other means of storage didn't exist. For instance, it was used to store meats at a time when no refrigeration was available. Meat was stacked into a pottery vessel, fat was put on the top as a sealant, and then the vessel was kept in a cold cellar for the winter. I personally use a small covered crock to store butter in my kitchen. We like soft butter, and pottery works perfect to keep butter at room temperature. I also have a small covered crock for my coffee beans that I grind in the morning for fresh coffee. I have a garlic keeper on the counter—a small crock with air holes that keeps garlic fresh for months. Our covered cookie canister keeps cookies moist and fresh for much longer than a plastic container, which builds up moisture that leads to mold. Sugar and flour I store in pottery in smaller quantities to ensure freshness. We have even made a large crock with holes on the bottom for potato and onion storage. This keeps the items from molding. I find moisture stays out and items stay fresh longer in my pottery storage. It is fun to look around my kitchen and realize just how much of my everyday staples are being stored in pottery.

What are the biggest differences between machine- and handmade wares?
First, it comes down to what the customer wants, which dictates what a potter makes. So, for instance, as trends change and people want square pieces, a company needs to meet consumer trends and use machines for, say, square wares. The differences are all about the personal touch—if it's there or not there—and the little quirks that make a piece handmade and come with heart. In everything we do, an artist's hands are part of the process. The biggest difference in having something handmade is that handiwork every step of the way. Now, as a business needs to stay alive, we—and others like us—might choose to press something that must be uniform, like sets of plates, because customers who love handmade pottery still want consistency on pieces like dinnerware. People today are accustomed to machine-made products, so we have to accommodate that. It also helps with speed. But even machine-molded clay needs to be hand trimmed and even hand decorated. That might not be the same in some larger factories that use machinery to do the entire process, but we promote potter-made pieces because each is slightly unique and different, just like people, and the meaning goes far deeper.

CHOOSING CLAY COOKWARE

The best part about clay is its incredible versatility. It can be fashioned into endless shapes and decorated with amazing glazes and colors. Individual pieces of cookware or bakeware can be used to create sumptuous dishes or entire meals. I particularly love making brownies in a huge rectangular clay dish that has handles, because the heft of the pan and the food within it help me carry the dish in and out of the oven without feeling unbalanced.

If I don't use a copper bowl to mix brownies and pancake batters, I'll use a big shiny white clay bowl. Well, it's shiny and white on the outside. The inside of the bowl has a lot of gray marks from using a handheld mixer. The rough, cheese-stained pizza stone, which was a wedding gift, keeps crusts soft and pliable (which John appreciates), and I really appreciate my covered ceramic baker for anything from cheesy potatoes for a potluck to apple cobbler.

I also use stoneware dishes to make the most of the foods at Thanksgiving. I think I'd fall over in shock if the green bean casserole came in something other than a round blue ceramic piece. My mom serves it piping hot, so the casserole needs to be housed in an exterior woven basket.

Whatever memories you treasure already, you can stock your kitchens to build new ones now. Here is the most common pottery to help you do it.

The Rectangular Baking Pan

While you can find bakeware pans in both rectangular and square shapes, rectangular ones will give you the most flexibility. Look for a sturdy pan with thick, wide handles molded as part of the body instead of riveted metal handles; you'll likely have fewer breakages if the pan slips in the sink. The bigger the piece, the heavier it will be, due to the amount of clay used to make it. Pick it up and carry it around the store to make sure you can handle it, because it won't be any lighter when it's full of food.

The Traditional Bowl

True stoneware bowls are hard to find because so many are made by machine or in factories and are not properly fired with a good, chip-resistant finish or glaze. Good bowls will have thicker walls—which can prevent breakage and withstand repeated microwave, dishwasher, and oven use—and glazed or rough bottoms, and they come in a dizzying array of sizes and glaze colors.

The Casserole Dish

The clay casserole dish is a common kitchen tool that can handle a wide variety of recipes. It's available in oval or round shapes with or without handles, and the sides are usually taller than those of regular square or rectangular pieces. Here is a bonus: The casserole dish has the visual appeal that makes going from oven to table a cinch.

The Pie Plate

The pie plate is a necessity for any serious baker, or at least one who likes to make pies, tarts, and crisps from scratch. (I wouldn't be a good daughter if I hadn't learned the secret of pie baking as one of the ways to a man's heart. Thanks, Mom and Dad!) Look for thick sides that can be smooth or slightly wavy. Pie plates come in either standard or deep-dish varieties with gently sloping sides. They can also be used to make quiches, frittatas, and brownies. Basically, anything delicious goes into a pie plate.

The Covered Pan

Similar to the casserole, square, or rectangular pan, the covered pan can come in multiple shapes (square, round, oval, or rectangular), but the bonus is that the lid slides into the lip of the pan. The seal is not airtight (nor is it meant to be), but it resolves a lot of issues when cooking or baking a dish that tends to bubble and spit juice into your oven. Additionally, since the lid is ceramic as well, you're essentially "baking" your dish a little more from the top and bottom.

The Butter Dish

This is a bit of a treat to have, but if you're stocking your kitchen, you're going to want a butter dish, which typically comes covered with a clay bottom and top. This is when the nature of ceramic really works for you. Ceramic is an insulator, not a conductor of heat, so the protection offered to your butter is profound, much like the way the ancients used to use pottery amphorae to keep sunlight from penetrating their wine and oil. The pottery prevents your butter from becoming rancid quickly.

The Pizza Stone

If your family enjoys baking a lot of pizza (homemade, frozen, or otherwise—no judgment here!), flat stoneware (sometimes called a pizza stone) is a fantastic way to go. It provides even heat to help cook the entire pizza, especially the center and at a rate faster than an aluminum pan. Be aware that these stones will stain, but it won't affect the performance or the taste. If you can, get one with clay handles connected to the stone itself, or a product that comes with a separate metal brace for carrying.

Clay reacts to extreme temperatures, and you have to be aware of that fact while cooking with it. With modern firing processes, pottery is dependable, and we know that the food-safe glazes and local clay used in modern wares are free from lead and made to last. (If you do have a very old piece, you may want to test the surface glaze for lead, which can be done by purchasing a lead detector kit. Simply buy online and swab!)

The advice I'm going to offer is particularly for traditional stoneware and basic ceramics, which are what most people have in their kitchen for everyday use. A word of caution: You're not going to bake a pie or mix cookie dough in porcelain, so please note that the advice and care suggestions given here are not necessarily the best choice for porcelain wares!

Caring for Clay Cookware

Caring for pottery bakeware and cookware is relatively easy because the glazes allow for intense scrubbing without any worry about taking off seasoning or scraping off metal fragments. You can scratch glazes with steel-wool pads and plenty of elbow grease, and you'll still have a fully operational piece of pottery. Because your clay bakeware is *not* nonstick, you'll always need to pregrease your piece before putting any food in for cooking or baking.

Greasing can involve any number of oils and fats, and whichever you choose should be spread thinly around the entire interior. Some greasing options include:

- Vegetable oil
- Crisco or other shortening
- Pam or other oil sprays
- Bacon fat or coconut oil (great for organic options!)

You may also choose to use a dusting of flour over the grease, which will absorb some of the oil and make for easy removal of the food.

Another common method is to both grease and flour the pan, and then add a piece of parchment paper cut to fit the bottom and the sides of the greased and floured pan. You can then grease and flour the parchment paper. This is usually the best for desserts like brownies, blondies, and other stickier and denser foods that need to be pulled out and cut with minimal leftover residue.

When using clay wares, remember these guidelines:

- Most ceramic cookware pieces are microwave safe. Some manufacturers do warn against using the microwave because their wares may heat the contents unevenly.
- Most ceramic cookware pieces are oven safe.
- Avoid extreme temperature changes, which may damage your piece. Don't take pottery from the oven and put it directly into the freezer or fill it with ice, and don't put a piece of pottery straight from the refrigerator into the oven—let it warm up a bit closer to room temperature first.
- Most ceramic cookware pieces are dishwasher safe. Be aware that ceramic wares can sometimes have unfinished bottoms. This does not typically create issues in dishwashers, but if you use abrasive dish soap, you may find the unfinished clay areas (parts not covered with glaze) to be a bit soft after a wash or see eventual cracks and pits.
- You may wish to "season" unglazed stoneware pieces using oils or fats (coconut oil, tallow, lard, and so on). This is best done by rubbing the oil/fat of your choice all over your unglazed stoneware and sticking it in an oven at 400°F to 425°F for 20 to 30 minutes. Remember to remove it safely with oven mitts! If you choose not to season, cook with fatty or oily foods during the first few uses.

Cleaning Clay Cookware by Hand

While most stoneware is dishwasher safe, you may prefer to hand-clean it—it's completely up to you. The beauty of today's ceramics is they can easily handle a long soaking. For stuck-on food, leave water in the pan overnight to soften. The next day, use a rag, scrub pads, or a tough bristle brush to clean off stubborn debris.

Porcelain and bone china have their own specific care needs because of their fragility, so I highly recommend you follow the manufacturer's guidelines. Usually these items cannot go in dishwashers because of the type of clay used, the thinness of the glaze, and the formation of the wares themselves. These specialty wares do require nonabrasive soap and gentle rags for washing and drying.

Here are some basic rules for cleaning stoneware, which is the majority of the ceramics available on the market today:

1. Always be sure the ceramic is cool enough to handle before cleaning to prevent personal injury or dropping the item.

2. Soak baked-on food with water and a bit of soap for as long as 24 hours before scrubbing off the debris.

3. Scrub with soft cloths, rough brushes, or even copper scrubbies.

4. Store on cool, dry shelves or inside drawers.

5. During the seasoning process, some rougher stoneware may require only some gentle brushing to clean, to ensure some of the natural food oils remain on the surface to help build the seasoning.

6. Unglazed and seasoned stoneware should not be washed with soap because it will strip away the seasoning.

Great Products

I'm a huge fan of using the following tried-and-true tools for cleaning and caring for stoneware:

1. Pampered Chef nylon pan scrapers

2. The Laundress copper cloth

A LIVING HISTORY

Do you know what amazes me? Pottery is the oldest cooking material known to man, and it's the simplest. I wonder if this is the genesis of the old adage: "If it's not broke, don't fix it!" Clay as cookware first worked ten thousand years ago on an island in Japan, and it's still used in every household today. Isn't that a lovely wonder?

And while some of us may not be able to make clay into useful or beautiful pieces, many of us can. The talent to take earth and make it usable, to change how we, as humans, were able to eat and prepare food, is in our bones. Clay sings to some and speaks to many of us. It is malleable and alive. The earth itself offered another way to nourish us from the very dust—and did so only once we were civilized enough to create the other necessary part of the equation: fire and flame.

Handcrafted pottery from start to finish—a tradition thousands of years old that still is used and creates usable wares. This feels like magic!

RECIPES

I've never claimed to be a chef, yet people constantly ask me for recipes. The ones I do have tend to be vintage, and there's real pleasure in making old recipes in pans that would have been suitable for them. And who knows more about using pans than chefs? I've asked some well-known cooks to offer favorite recipes, along with their thoughts on wares. I've also provided some of my family's favorites and my own old-school, tried-and-true recipes, too!

The recipes do mention particular cookware that will work well when it makes sense to be precise, but the final choice is up to the individual home cook. Enjoy playing in the kitchen!

MOTHER'S BUTTERMILK PANCAKES

By Lisa Schroeder ● **Makes 16 pancakes**

Lisa Schroeder is the executive chef and owner of Mother's Bistro & Bar in downtown Portland, Oregon. She's also the author of the cookbook *Mother's Best*, a mother, grandmother, and mother hen to more than seventy-five employees. In 1992, while juggling a marketing career, catering, and raising her daughter, Lisa realized that there was no place that served the kind of food she would make if she had the time: slow-cooked dishes made with love. (You can find Lisa's "Love Notes" next to each recipe in her cookbook, too!) She spent the next eight years working toward opening such a restaurant. Touring Italy, Spain, Morocco, and Switzerland, she gained an understanding of regional cuisine and indigenous foods, affirming her belief that some of the best meals of a country are found in its homes, made by its mothers.

In addition to offering a menu of refined versions of traditional home-cooked dishes, each month Lisa celebrates the cuisine of a different mother, lovingly referred to as the "Mother of the Month," or MOM.

3 cups all-purpose flour
(see Love Note A)

1½ teaspoons baking soda

3 teaspoons baking powder

¼ cup sugar

½ teaspoon salt

4½ cups buttermilk

3 large eggs

6 tablespoons (¾ stick) unsalted butter, melted, plus softened or whipped butter, for serving

Vegetable oil or clarified butter, for brushing the griddle or pan

Pure maple syrup, for serving

1 Preheat the oven to 200°F.

2 In a large bowl, whisk together the flour, baking soda, baking powder, sugar, and salt.

3 In a medium bowl, whisk together the buttermilk and eggs.

4 While gently stirring, pour the buttermilk mixture into the flour mixture. Mix just until combined; overmixing will activate the gluten in the flour and the pancakes will be chewy, not fluffy. A few lumps are okay; if you find pockets of flour bigger than a dime, smash them against the side of the bowl to break them apart without stirring further.

Pour in the melted butter and gently mix just until incorporated. (Sometimes melted butter solidifies when added to cold ingredients. Adding it now helps it disperse evenly in the batter and smooth out some of the lumps.)

5 Place a griddle (see Love Note B) or wide (preferably 14-inch) sauté pan over medium heat for several minutes. If using an electric griddle, set the heat to 350°F. Sprinkle the griddle with a few drops of water; they should bounce around before evaporating. If they sizzle away quickly, the heat is too high. If they just sit there and slowly steam, the heat is too low.

6 When the griddle is properly heated, brush it with oil or clarified butter, then wipe with a paper towel so it's evenly greased. (Big spots of oil or butter will promote uneven browning and your pancakes will have dark and light spots. If you have a nonstick griddle, you can skip the oil/butter and wiping step.)

7 Use a 4-ounce (½-cup) ladle (see Love Note C) to pour several 5- or 6-inch pools of batter onto the griddle, 1 or 2 inches apart.

8 Cook until bubbles begin to pop on the surface of the pancakes, the edges look a little dry, and the underside is golden, about 2 minutes (try not to flip the pancakes before they're ready, because the more you flip them back and forth the less fluffy they will be). Flip the pancakes and cook until they are cooked through, about 1 minute more. (If the undersides of the pancakes are browning or burning before the surface of the pancakes gets a chance to form bubbles and dry out, the heat is too high. If it's taking much longer than 2 or 3 minutes for the bubbles to form, the heat is too low.)

9 Repeat with the remaining batter. Keep the pancakes warm on a heat-safe platter or sheet pan in the oven.

10 Serve topped with softened or whipped butter and maple syrup.

LOVE NOTES

A While some people like their pancakes thick and rib sticking, I like mine thin and light, so I can eat more and they won't sit in my stomach like a lump. But it's all a matter of opinion. Try cooking up 2 pancakes and see how you like them. If you want yours a little thicker, stir in ½ cup to 1 cup more flour.

B Old-fashioned ovens often had a griddle (flat cooking surface) built right into the cooktop. That's not a common feature in ranges these days. Luckily there are many different griddles you can buy to put on your stove, from heavy cast iron to lightweight nonstick aluminum. Some sit on just one burner and some are elongated to stretch across two. There are also electric models that plug in, sit on the countertop, and let you set a precise temperature. My preference is the old-school, heavy cast-iron griddle.

C Ladles come in all sorts of standard sizes, from 1 ounce to 12 ounces, which helps measure as you serve. At Mother's we use a 6-ounce ladle, which holds about $^3/_4$ cup batter. That makes a big plate-size pancake, but it's likely too big to be practical at home. Instead, use a 4-ounce ($^1/_2$-cup) ladle, which makes 6-inch pancakes. To find out how many ounces your ladle is, fill it with water, pour the water into a dry measuring cup, and read the results. If you don't have the right ladle, use a dry measuring cup to scoop the batter.

Variations: With a little addition and subtraction, you can completely change the flavor of your flapjacks. Add-ins like nuts and berries are usually dropped onto each pancake after you spoon the batter on the griddle. Wait until the batter has begun to set but is still wet. Sprinkle the ingredients evenly over the surface, then flip.

PUMPKIN CRANBERRY BREAD

Makes 1 loaf

My grandmother Betty was one of those women who would wear pearls every day without ever appearing pretentious. They fit her exactly: cultured, poised, lovely, and elegant. She also once climbed into a hot tub wearing an evening dress—completely sober—at the after-party of my parents' wedding (I know because there is photographic evidence), and she could cook the best sloppy Joes ever.

This isn't the sloppy Joe recipe, though. This is her quick bread. It is a treat, and it has won awards, which is saying something because one of those times it came straight out of the freezer to the judge's table with only 30 minutes to thaw! (This delicious bread does freeze outlandishly well.)

Chocolate chips can be substituted for the cranberries, of course.

Cooking spray or butter, for the pan

3 cups all-purpose flour, plus more for the pan

1 tablespoon plus 2 teaspoons pumpkin pie spice

2 teaspoons baking soda

1½ teaspoons table salt

3 cups sugar

One 15-ounce can pumpkin puree

4 large eggs

1 cup vegetable oil

⅓ cup orange juice or water

1 cup fresh, frozen, or dried cranberries

1 Preheat the oven to 350°F. Grease and flour a 5 × 9-inch pan, a 4 × 8-inch pan, or 4 mini loaf pans. Or use a 12-inch cast-iron skillet.

2 In a large bowl, combine the flour, pumpkin pie spice, baking soda, and salt. In another large bowl, using a spoon or a mixer, mix the sugar, pumpkin puree, eggs, oil, and orange juice until well blended.

3 Pour the wet mixture into the dry mixture and mix until just blended (don't overmix). Fold in the cranberries.

4 Pour the batter into the prepared pan. Bake as follows; the bread is done when a toothpick inserted into the center comes out clean:

5 × 9-INCH PAN: 60 to 65 minutes

4 × 8-INCH PAN: 55 to 60 minutes

MINI LOAF PANS: 55 minutes

5 Let the loaf cool, then serve at room temperature.

6 Store up to 4 days in an airtight container at room temperature. To freeze, wrap first in plastic wrap, then aluminum foil. The loaf will keep up to 1 year; defrost for at least 45 minutes before serving.

FRIED HALLOUMI WITH HEMP AND SESAME SEEDS

Makes 14 servings

I'm a Wisconsin girl through and through, and I think fried cheese curds have been part of my diet since I could chew. Sometime later, I discovered the true magic of frying cheese, especially the delicious salty ridiculousness of halloumi—my all-time favorite!—in an iron skillet.

I discovered this combo by accident when after roasting some hemp, sesame, and sunflower seeds for another recipe, I was too lazy to clean the skillet thoroughly. Plus I figured, *That's good oil! Don't waste it!* Let's face it—fried cheese is pretty darn good any way you make it, but those deeply crispy little seeds I'd left in the skillet made it even better. So leave the seeds in the pan!

1/2 pound halloumi

2 tablespoons olive oil

1 tablespoon raw hemp seeds

1 tablespoon raw sesame seeds

1 tablespoon raw sunflower seeds

1 Slice the cheese into 1/4-inch-thick slabs, then cut each slab in half. You will end up with about 28 slices.

2 Heat the oil in a large cast-iron skillet over medium heat. Add the seeds and toast them until medium to dark brown in color, stirring often.

3 Evenly place the cheese slices in the skillet and cook until the cheese starts to bubble slightly, then turn them over with a rubber spatula and cook the other side until toasted and dark brown over most of the surface. Some of the white of the cheese will still be visible on both sides of the cheese.

4 Serve the cheese hot on its own, with crackers, or on top of a salad made of sturdy greens, such as cabbage, collards, or dandelion greens.

5 Store leftover halloumi in an airtight container in the refrigerator for up to 2 days.

MY DAD'S CORNED BEEF DIP

Makes 2 cups

I'm not sure if this particular dip is a Wisconsin thing, but I have yet to see it served outside basement rec rooms, where Christmas parties in the cold month of December are in full swing and every host has a bowl of this dip sitting on a sideboard alongside Wild Cat.* It can be served as a warm dip with the addition of sauerkraut, but I've personally never done that, so I can't speak to it. I watched my parents, Allie and Diane, make this for more holiday events than I can count. The ingredients are few, and it's important to get the right combination so no one of them overpowers another. There's a lot of taste-testing involved. And this was yet another instance where I was taught by "feel, look, and taste" rather than an actual recipe. You may find that you like your dip to be more savory and will add more onion or salt and pepper. There's no wrong way.

One 8-ounce package
cream cheese

1/2 cup sour cream

1/3 cup minced Vidalia or
other sweet onion

Two 2-ounce packages thin-sliced
corned beef, chopped into 1/4-inch
pieces

Salt and freshly ground black pepper

1 Cream together the cream cheese and sour cream until fully blended. A mixer helps if you're making a double or triple batch. Add the onions and mix to distribute them well. Fold in the corn beef and gently combine until fully mixed.

2 Add salt and pepper to taste, stir, taste again, and adjust to add more of any ingredient you like. Cover and chill until serving.

3 Serve cold with crackers or a baguette of your choice.

4 Store leftover dip in an airtight container in the refrigerator for up to 1 week.

*Wild Cat is an appetizer that's popular in Wisconsin and elsewhere in the Midwest. It's mostly brought out for Christmas and involves a cracker or piece of brown bread heaped with plenty of good-quality, absolutely raw ground beef topped with salt, pepper, and raw onion.

SECRET FAMILY POTATO SALAD

Makes 10 servings

When I first asked for this recipe, my father had me make it with him, apparently assuming I'd be able to commit it to memory. I was in middle school and definitely did not memorize it. Then, when I was older, I finally had him recite it to me so I could write it down. It came with fantastically unusable instructions, such as "a minuscule bit of milk" and "Beau Monde—a generous amount!" and "just a tiny part of sour cream." There was even a mention of "celery sauce," which I've never used in the recipe because I can't find it.

After many years of married life, and lots of potato salad, I've been able to actually get it down in usable and passable directions. It is wildly successful at every picnic—now people actually request I bring it as my dish to pass. Hint: Don't ever forget the Beau Monde!

Note there is some chilling time required for the potatoes and eggs, and again when the recipe is complete.

5 large red-skinned potatoes, unpeeled	1½ teaspoons ground mustard
5 large eggs	¼ teaspoon salt
⅔ cup Hellmann's mayonnaise	¼ teaspoon freshly ground black pepper
1 teaspoon sour cream	1 teaspoon celery seeds
½ teaspoon milk	2 tablespoons Beau Monde seasoning (or more to taste!)
¼ cup minced Vidalia onion	1 tablespoon sweet paprika
⅓ cup finely diced celery	

1 In a large pot over medium-high heat, cover the potatoes with water and bring to a boil. Cook until the potatoes are soft enough that a fork goes in easily, typically 10 to 15 minutes after the boil starts. Remove from the heat, drain, and refrigerate immediately. Chill for at least 3 hours or overnight. To speed the chilling process, add the potatoes to a bowl of ice water for an hour. If using an ice bath, you should be able to peel the eggs and potatoes immediately without chilling in the refrigerator.

2 While the potatoes are cooking, place the eggs in a medium saucepan and add water to cover the eggs by 1 inch. Bring to a boil and leave the eggs in the boiling water for 8 minutes. Drain the eggs and refrigerate immediately. Chill in the refrigerator for at least 3 hours or overnight. Or chill first in a bowl of ice water (see step 1).

3 When the eggs and potatoes are thoroughly chilled, peel both the eggs and the potatoes and cut them into bite-size chunks. Place them in a large bowl.

4 In a medium bowl, combine the mayonnaise, sour cream, milk, onion, celery, mustard, salt, pepper, celery seeds, and Beau Monde. Add the mayonnaise mixture to the potatoes and eggs and gently fold until the potatoes and eggs are coated. Taste and adjust any of the seasonings to your preference.

5 Cover and refrigerate for 1 to 3 hours before serving.

6 Top with the paprika and serve chilled.

7 Store leftover potato salad in an airtight container in the refrigerator for up to 5 days.

MATZO BALL SOUP

By Natasha Feldman ● Makes 4 servings

✖✖✖✖✖

While studying Shakespearean acting in London, Natasha Feldman quickly discovered she had greater pleasure looking at stacks of walnut-speckled brownies and wheels of cheese in Borough Market than she did taking a bow at the end of a show. Yahoo! aired Natasha's first cooking show, which she coproduced, directed, and hosted. Since then, she has been both in front of and behind the camera, spreading her enthusiasm for simple cooking and great food. You can watch her host her Food Network original online show, *Craving Healthy*.

STOCK

1 chicken, cut into 8 parts
(make sure the butcher gives you
the back and neck)

3 carrots, halved

1 yellow onion, quartered

1 parsnip, halved

2 celery ribs, halved

1 bunch fresh dill

1 bunch fresh parsley

1 bay leaf

1 teaspoon black peppercorns

1 tablespoon kosher salt, plus more
to taste

MATZO BALLS

4 large eggs

1/4 cup schmaltz (rendered chicken fat),
or 2 parts shortening and 1 part mild oil

1 cup matzo meal

1/4 cup chicken stock

2 tablespoons peeled grated fresh ginger

2 tablespoons chopped fresh dill

1/4 teaspoon ground nutmeg

1/2 teaspoon garlic powder

2 teaspoons kosher salt

1/2 teaspoon freshly ground black pepper

1/2 teaspoon table salt

TO SERVE

Freshly ground black pepper

Chopped fresh parsley

Chopped fresh dill

1 To make the soup, fill a stockpot with water. Add the chicken, carrots, onion, parsnip, celery, dill, parsley, bay leaf, and peppercorns and bring to a boil over medium-high heat. Reduce to a simmer and cook slowly for 1½ hours. Remove the chicken from the pot and set aside to cool.

2 When the chicken is cool enough to handle, separate the meat from the bones. Throw the bones back into the pot, place the chicken in a covered container, and refrigerate.

3 Simmer the stock for a few more hours, until it's a luscious golden color.

4 While the stock is simmering, make the matzo mixture. In a large bowl, combine the eggs, schmaltz, matzo meal, stock (using fresh stock from the pot), ginger, dill, nutmeg, garlic powder, and kosher salt. Mix gently but thoroughly, cover the bowl, and refrigerate a few hours, until firm.

5 Back to the stock! Carefully strain the liquid into another large pot and discard the vegetables and bones. Add the kosher salt and pepper. If you're not using the stock right away for the matzo ball soup, cover and refrigerate it for up to 3 days.

6 Bring a large pot of water to a boil over medium-high heat and add the table salt.

7 Using wet hands, form the matzo mixture into about 10 balls roughly the size of a golf ball.

8 Carefully drop them in the boiling water and reduce the heat to a simmer. Cook for about 30 minutes, until the balls float, then drain.

9 Serve the matzo balls in the stock. Garnish each bowl with pepper and a sprinkling of parsley and dill.

10 Store leftover soup in an airtight container in the refrigerator for up to 3 days.

SPICY CHICKPEA SOUP

By Natasha Feldman ● Makes 6 servings

A bright and colorful soup, this one is healthy and also a great replacement for chili. The flavor is layered with all kinds of savory deliciousness. Natasha is all about providing recipes that can be made at home but look restaurant ready, and this soup fits her philosophy precisely.

2 tablespoons olive oil

1 yellow onion, finely chopped

3 garlic cloves, minced

2 carrots, finely diced

1 red bell pepper, cored, seeded, and cut into ½-inch chunks

1 cup peeled ½-inch-diced sweet potato

2 celery ribs, cut into ¼-inch dice

½ tablespoon smoked paprika

1 teaspoon garlic powder

1 teaspoon dried oregano

1 teaspoon onion powder

1 teaspoon dried basil

½ teaspoon dried thyme

1 teaspoon kosher salt

1 teaspoon freshly ground black pepper

¼ teaspoon ground cayenne

2½ cups canned stewed tomatoes (about 1½ 14.5-ounce cans)

One 15-ounce can chickpeas, drained and rinsed

1 quart chicken or vegetable stock

½ cup heavy cream

2 cups fresh spinach

1 In a large Dutch oven, heat the oil over medium-low heat. Add the onion and sauté until aromatic. Add the garlic, carrots, bell pepper, sweet potato, and celery and cook for 5 minutes, stirring frequently. Add all the seasonings and cook for about 3 minutes, until fragrant. Add the tomatoes, chickpeas, and stock, stir well, and simmer until the vegetables are soft, about 30 minutes.

2 Taking care not to burn yourself with the hot liquid, pour half the soup into a blender to create a creamy texture. Return the blended soup to the pot and stir to combine.

3 Add the cream and spinach just before serving. The spinach will wilt almost instantly.

4 Serve very warm.

5 Store leftover soup in an airtight container in the refrigerator for up to 3 days.

STUFFED PEPPERS

Makes 6 servings

What is it about stuffed peppers that makes me think of fall? Is it the bountiful harvest vibe or the smell of roasting peppers? Or is it because one never really makes this in the heat of summer? Frankly, it's too hot for hot stuffed peppers in July when peppers start to be in season.

In any case, I've poached this particular dish from a stash of tried-and-true recipes belonging to my mother, Diane. I don't know if she knows where it came from, but it was a staple of my childhood and taught me that green peppers can turn sweet with the right amount of cooking. I make this in copper in the oven at home and over a campfire when we are at rendezvous events and living in tents. Whether in an oven or over a flame, this recipe has never failed me.

6 green bell peppers, halved, cored, and seeded

Table salt

1 pound ground beef

2 tablespoons chopped onion

1 teaspoon kosher salt

1/8 teaspoon garlic salt

1 cup cooked rice (you can use Minute rice, but if you have the time to cook real rice for 30 minutes, do it!)

One 15-ounce can tomato sauce

1 cup shredded Cheddar cheese (optional)

1 Preheat the oven to 350°F.

2 In a large pot, bring the peppers and 5 cups salted water to a low boil over medium heat until the peppers begin to soften, 10 to 15 minutes.

3 Place the softened peppers in a shallow 9 × 11-inch baking dish. Set aside.

4 In a large skillet, cook the beef and onion together over medium heat until the beef is brown and the onion translucent. Pour off all but a tablespoon of the fat.

5 In a large bowl, combine the meat and onion with the kosher salt, garlic salt, rice, and tomato sauce. Divide the mixture among the pepper halves.

6 Cover (aluminum foil is fine!) and bake for 45 minutes. Remove the cover and bake 15 minutes more. Sprinkle cheese, if using, on top of each pepper half and broil for a minute or two, until melted and browning. Serve very warm.

7 Store leftover peppers in an airtight container in the refrigerator for up to 3 days.

STUFFED BEEF TENDERLOIN

Makes 6 servings

This is a vintage recipe from the early 1900s that I found in an old newspaper shortly after I was married. I clipped it, wrote it out on one of those note cards we used in school, and laminated it. I saved the card in a little wooden recipe box that I'd found at a secondhand store. The box was decorated with Swedish stencils, and the word RECIPES was hand labeled with a Sharpie. The recipes in that box were all that would fit in our tiny newlywed apartment—no space for cookbooks. I always promised myself I'd paint over the stencils and scrawled writing on the box, but after thirteen years of marriage, I still haven't!

Anyway, this recipe has carried me through countless dinner parties, because it never fails. Though it sounds a little finicky in terms of preparation, it really isn't. Once you've tried it, it'll be one of the easiest fancy meals you've ever made. You can even play around with the herbs, exchanging the basil for dill or sage if you wish. It's pretty foolproof.

I serve this in messy slices alongside salad of any kind.

4 tablespoons (1/2 stick) unsalted butter

1 medium yellow onion, finely chopped

1/2 cup minced celery

4 ounces white button mushrooms, trimmed and thinly sliced (1/2 cup)

2 cups bread crumbs (I like to use toast torn up into 1/2-inch chunks, or even crushed unseasoned salad croutons)

1/2 teaspoon kosher salt

1/8 teaspoon freshly ground black pepper

1/2 teaspoon dried basil

1/8 teaspoon dried parsley

3 pounds beef tenderloin roast, butterflied (see Note)

6 slices bacon

1 Preheat the oven to 350°F.

2 Melt the butter in a medium saucepan over medium heat. Add the onion, celery, and mushrooms and sauté until the onion is transparent, about 5 minutes. Set aside to cool.

3 In a medium bowl, combine the bread crumbs, salt, pepper, basil, and parsley. Add the reserved vegetables and mix to combine.

4 Place the meat in a medium casserole dish and put the stuffing into the butterfly pocket. Roll up the meat and close it with toothpicks or kitchen twine. Place the seam of

the meat roll facing up. Lay the bacon slices diagonally over the seam, lined up next to one another. Tuck any excess bacon length under the tenderloin roll.

5 Bake uncovered until a meat thermometer registers 150°F, about 1 hour for medium rare.

6 Remove the toothpicks or twine, cut the roll into 1-inch slices, and serve hot.

7 Store leftover tenderloin in an airtight container for up to 3 days.

Note: Your butcher can butterfly the tenderloin, but if you're doing it yourself, simply cut it lengthwise but not all the way through, as if you were cutting open a baguette but leaving a hinge.

KNOLL FAMILY PIEROGI

Makes 8 servings

➤➤➤◄◄

My grandma Stella was the matriarch of my father's family. She presided over ten children on the farm (my dad was second youngest) and whatever Polish nuns and cousins came for the summer. I have no idea what the nuns did, but my cousins were definitely put to work on the farm. My grandfather was known for raising honeybees—and for putting a ridiculous number of Christmas lights on his pine trees for the holidays.

My dad and his siblings were raised in a Polish-speaking farmhouse, so I grew up hearing Polish words dropped into conversation, understanding them through context and thinking all was good until I was told I shouldn't use words like *studabubba* in proper company. (In my family, it was loosely translated as "old bag" or "hag," though it was used with affection.) I remember driving home from college on cold January weekends to help the group of female cousins and aunts make hundreds of pierogi from scratch (the gender line was strictly observed with this kitchen project). But I swear someone would tip off the men, because they'd always show up just in time to snitch fresh ones as soon as they were done.

A personal disclaimer: I have inherited multiple recipes for the dough and filling from aunts, great-aunts, and cousins. There are at least five dough variations in circulation and just as many fillings—you can use sauerkraut or meat or even vegetables! For this recipe, I'm using Grandma Stella's dough and Great-Aunt Evelyn's filling—I'll handle any intrafamily debate later.

These freeze really well! See the instructions in the Note on page 218.

DOUGH

4 large eggs

5 cups all-purpose flour, plus more for rolling out the dough

2 teaspoons salt

½ cup shortening

FILLING

Two 12-ounce containers dry-curd cottage cheese (sometimes called farmer's cheese or baker's cheese; see Note)

1 large egg

¾ cup finely minced Vidalia or other sweet onion

1 teaspoon salt

1 teaspoon freshly ground black pepper

Unsalted butter, for frying

1 In a medium bowl, beat the eggs until very well frothed.

2 In a large bowl, mix the flour and salt. Form the flour into a mound and create a well in the middle of it. Add the eggs and shortening. Mix very well together with a spoon, then knead with your hands, adding tablespoons of water one at a time until the dough is soft, pliable, and stretchy. The amount of water will depend on the weather, the grain of your flour, and experience. This step might take a little practice.

3 Turn out the dough onto a lightly floured surface. Knead for 10 minutes, then let rest on the counter for 30 minutes. You can leave bare or cover with a cotton towel.

4 Meanwhile, make the filling: In a large bowl, combine the cottage cheese, egg, onion, salt, and pepper. Set aside until the dough is ready for rolling.

5 Place a large pot on the stove, fill it with water, and bring it to a boil over high heat.

6 On a floured surface, roll out the dough to $1/8$ inch thick. Use a 4-inch cookie cutter (or the edge of a large drinking glass or ramekin) to cut circles from the dough.

7 Place 2 tablespoons of filling in the center of a dough circle, then fold the circle over to create a half-moon shape. Press the edges of the dough together to seal them so the filling doesn't escape during boiling. Sometimes folding one edge over the other and pressing helps. Set it aside while you finish filling and sealing the rest.

8 Working in batches so as not to crowd the pot, use a slotted spoon to slip the pierogi into the boiling water. Boil for 7 to 10 minutes, until they float. Place on a clean cotton towel to dry as you finish them.

9 In a large cast-iron skillet, melt 1 teaspoon of butter over medium-high heat. Add a single layer of pierogi (don't crowd the pan) and fry until golden on both sides, about 4 to 6 minutes per side. Repeat with more butter to fry each batch. Serve hot.

10 Store leftover pierogi in an airtight container in the refrigerator for up to 4 days.

Notes:

To freeze, place the pierogi on a sheet pan after step 7 and place in the freezer. When frozen solid, remove to a freezer bag and store for up to 4 months. When you want to cook them, boil them straight from the freezer (they will take about 10 minutes), then fry.

If you cannot find the right cheese, make your own. Pour 16 ounces of full-fat cottage cheese in a colander and gently rinse until the water runs clear. Spread the curds in a single layer on a clean cotton cloth and let them air-dry until the curds are no longer wet to the touch, about 1 hour.

BEEF BOURGUIGNON

By Beth Le Manach ● **Makes 6 servings**

Beth Le Manach has been cooking and entertaining for more than twenty years, and she is the creator of a popular, award-winning video blog on YouTube, *Entertaining with Beth*. Her recipes are often inspired by her yearly adventures in France (and her artistic French husband!) and the large vegetable garden she cultivates at her Los Angeles home.

Beth's favorite heirloom piece of cookware is her cast-iron skillet, which she calls "the most versatile pan around" and the one she couldn't do without. She purchased two at once so she could pass one down to both of her daughters. To Beth, real heirloom cookware is meant to be both used *and* cherished.

½ cup plus 1 tablespoon all-purpose flour

3 pounds chuck beef (stew meat), cut into 1-inch chunks

Kosher salt and freshly ground black pepper

1 tablespoon olive oil, plus more as needed

6 slices applewood smoked bacon, cut into bite-size pieces

1 cup ¼-inch-diced yellow onion

3 carrots, cut into 1-inch chunks on the bias

3 cups red wine (such as Côtes du Rhône or Pinot Noir)

3 cups beef stock

¼ cup tomato paste

2 garlic cloves, minced

2 teaspoons dried thyme

1 bay leaf

2 tablespoons unsalted butter

8 ounces white button mushrooms, trimmed and halved vertically (1 cup)

1 cup frozen pearl onions

¼ cup roughly chopped fresh parsley

2 French baguettes, for serving

1 Put ½ cup flour into a bowl. Season the beef with 1 teaspoon each of the salt and the pepper. Dredge the beef through the flour to coat it lightly. Set aside.

2 In a large Dutch oven, heat the 1 tablespoon oil. Add the bacon and sauté until crispy. Use a slotted spoon to remove the bacon to a paper-towel-lined plate. Add the onion and carrots to the bacon fat in the pot and sauté until the onion is slightly caramelized and the carrots are slightly tender, about 10 minutes. Remove the vegetables to a medium bowl using a slotted spoon and set aside.

3 Add a drizzle of oil to the pot if it's dry. Turn the heat to medium high and add the beef in a single layer, working in batches so as not to crowd the beef. Sear the beef on all sides until golden brown, about 8 minutes total. Remove the seared beef to a plate as you continue with the batches. *Do not rinse out the pot.* All those drippings equal flavor!

4 Preheat the oven to 325°F.

5 With the heat on medium high, deglaze the pot with the wine. Use a wooden spoon to loosen the crispy bits on the bottom of the pan. Add the stock, tomato paste, garlic, thyme, bay leaf, 1 teaspoon salt, and a few grindings of pepper. Whisk to combine. Return the sautéed carrots and onion, beef, and bacon to the pot.

6 Cover the pot and cook the stew in the oven for 2 hours.

7 When the stew has about 30 minutes left to cook, in a small sauté pan over medium heat, melt 1 tablespoon of the butter. Add the mushrooms and season with salt and pepper. Sauté the mushrooms until browned and tender, about 5 minutes. Add the mushrooms and their pan drippings to the stew and then the pearl onions. Return the stew to the oven.

8 Meanwhile prepare a slurry: In a small bowl, combine the 1 tablespoon flour with 2 tablespoons water and whisk together with a fork until smooth.

9 At the 2-hour mark, remove the stew from the oven and uncover it. Test the beef for tenderness by separating the meat with two forks. If it does not fall apart tenderly, cover the pot and return the stew to the oven for 15 minutes. If you need more time, check every 5 minutes after that.

10 Uncover the pot, place it over high heat, stir in the slurry, and bring to a boil. Simmer for 1 minute, until the sauce has thickened up a bit. Stir in the remaining 1 tablespoon of butter to create a smooth and velvety finish.

11 Ladle into bowls, top with fresh parsley, and serve with crusty French baguettes.

12 This stew is great when made ahead! Let it cool completely, then transfer to an airtight container and refrigerate for up to 4 days. Reheat in a covered pan over medium-low heat until heated through; it will start thick but thin out as it heats.

"HOBO" DINNER

Makes 4 servings

One of my easiest and fastest recipes, this is one that the kids can help with from age one onward, and they generally eat it because they've made it (such a reward to get the toddler to eat onions and cooked potatoes, for some reason!). Plus, it's delicious! I believe the "hobo" part comes from the fact that it's all packed together in a foil packet and could be cooked over an open fire pretty much anywhere in the world. It's easy to play with variations as well; try different types of meat and vegetables to your heart's content!

1 pound ground beef

2 russet potatoes, unpeeled, cut into thin strips

1 medium yellow onion, cut into ¼-inch-thick half-moon slices

4 carrots, cut into thin strips

2 tablespoons unsalted butter

1 teaspoon kosher salt, plus more for serving

1 teaspoon freshly ground black pepper, plus more for serving

Ketchup, for serving

1 Preheat the oven to 350°F.

2 Divide the ground beef into 4 patties and place each one on a 10 × 12-inch foil rectangle. Divide the potatoes, onion, and carrots evenly among the foil rectangles and place next to the beef. Place ½ tablespoon butter on each pile of vegetables and season everything liberally with salt and pepper. Fold the foil into packets that won't leak: Raise the ends, tuck them over the food, and roll the tops tight.

3 Place the packets directly on the oven rack and cook for 40 minutes, until the potatoes and carrots are tender and the meat is browned. (These packets can also be cooked on an outdoor grill or over an open fire on an elevated grate.)

4 Serve warm with ketchup and additional salt and pepper.

5 Store leftover hobo packets in their foil wrapping in the refrigerator for up to 2 days.

COQ AU VIN

By Beth Le Manach ● **Makes 6 servings**

I used to think coq au vin would be hard to make, so I didn't tackle it for years!
Even though there are a lot of steps to making coq au vin—a daunting challenge for
anyone with young kids—it's always worth it. I've made it in copper and cast iron
and it's come out well both ways.

½ teaspoon plus 1 tablespoon
unsalted butter

7 slices applewood smoked bacon,
cut into small pieces

6 skin-on, bone-in chicken legs

2 teaspoons kosher salt

2 teaspoons freshly ground black pepper

2 carrots, cut into 1-inch chunks

¾ cup frozen pearl onions

½ teaspoon dried thyme

⅓ cup cognac

½ cup full-bodied red wine

1 cup chicken stock

2 garlic cloves

2 tablespoons tomato paste

1 bay leaf

3 dashes of Worcestershire sauce

2 tablespoons cornstarch

12 ounces white button mushrooms,
trimmed and quartered (1½ cups)

1 tablespoon chopped fresh thyme,
to garnish

Mashed potatoes and/or crusty
French bread, for serving

1 In a large stockpot over medium-high heat, melt the ½ teaspoon butter. Add the
bacon and sauté until crispy. Use a slotted spoon to transfer the bacon to a paper-towel-
lined plate. Leave the fat in the pan.

2 Season the chicken legs on both sides with 1 teaspoon of the salt and 1 teaspoon of
the pepper. Add the chicken to the bacon fat and cook on both sides over medium heat
until browned, 3 to 5 minutes per side. Transfer to a plate to rest.

3 Add the carrots and onions and cook in the chicken fat until browned and tender,
about 10 minutes. Add the dried thyme.

4 Turn the heat to low, add the cognac and wine, and stir. Increase the heat to medium
and add the stock, garlic, tomato paste, bay leaf, and the remaining 1 teaspoon of salt. Stir
to combine. Add 3 dashes of Worcestershire sauce and stir to incorporate.

5 Preheat the oven to 350°F.

6 Create a slurry by combining the cornstarch with 2 tablespoons of water in a small bowl. Whisk together with a fork to combine. Add the slurry to the pot, stir, and bring to a boil. Lower the heat to a simmer and cook, stirring, about 15 minutes.

7 Place the chicken back into the pot, skin side up. Cover with a lid or aluminum foil. Place in the oven and bake for 25 minutes.

8 Meanwhile, in a large skillet over medium heat, sauté the mushrooms in the remaining 1 tablespoon of butter until browned, about 7 minutes.

9 Add the mushrooms to the pot and stir them in. Cover and bake for 20 minutes or until the chicken's internal temperature is at 165°F.

10 Uncover, garnish with fresh thyme, and bring to the table! Serve with mashed potatoes and/or crusty French bread.

11 Store leftover coq au vin in an airtight container in the refrigerator for up to 2 days.

SOUTHERN FRIED RABBIT

By John Gorham • Makes 6 servings

John Gorham is co-owner and executive chef of iconic Portland, Oregon, restaurants Toro Bravo, Tasty n Sons, Tasty n Alder, and Plaza del Toro; co-owner of Mediterranean Exploration Company, BYH Burgers, and Shalom Y'all; and founder of the La Ruta PDX gastronomic festival. A chef of the people, John celebrates a range of global cuisines at his influential restaurants.

In John's words: *When you have a good cast-iron pan, you covet the seasoning on it. I've only had the seasoning get ruined once. It was a birthday party a couple years ago. We had a caterer at our house and they baked oysters in it with salt. I got it out the next day and it was rusty and stripped to the plain steel. It took about two years to get it back to its nonstick seasoning.*

Fried rabbit is a must for cast iron.

BUTTERMILK BRINE

1 quart buttermilk

2 tablespoons sugar

¼ cup kosher salt

2 bay leaves

Juice of 2 lemons

1 teaspoon garlic powder

1 teaspoon onion powder

½ teaspoon ground cayenne

½ teaspoon freshly ground black pepper

1 rabbit, broken down into 12 pieces

RABBIT DREDGE

1¼ pounds all-purpose flour

1¼ tablespoons baking powder

¾ cup cornstarch

2 tablespoons sweet paprika

¾ tablespoon mild curry powder

1½ teaspoons freshly ground black pepper, plus more to taste

3 tablespoons kosher salt, plus more to taste

¾ tablespoon ground cayenne

FOR FRYING

1 quart canola oil

1 pound lard

1 Combine all the brine ingredients in a large container with a lid. Whisk thoroughly until blended. Soak the rabbit pieces in the brine overnight in the refrigerator.

2 Combine the dredge ingredients in a very large bowl or container.

3 Toss the rabbit pieces thoroughly in the dredge. Set aside on a sheet pan.

4 In a Dutch oven or very large cast-iron skillet with 3-inch-high (or higher) sides, combine the oil and lard. Heat it over high heat to 350°F.

5 Working in batches as needed so as not to crowd the pot, fry the rabbit until the pieces are dark caramel in color and a meat thermometer registers an internal temperature of 150°F.

6 Season with salt and pepper and serve very warm.

7 Store leftover rabbit in an airtight container in the refrigerator for 1 day.

RHUBARB PIE

By Mary Sue Milliken ● Makes one 10-inch pie

Mary Sue Milliken is a renowned chef, cookbook author, and television personality. A pioneer of world cuisine since the 1980s, Mary Sue is most notably recognized as a preeminent ambassador of modern Mexican cuisine, along with her business partner of thirty-five years, chef Susan Feniger, with their Border Grill Restaurants. She has coauthored five cookbooks and costarred in nearly 400 episodes of the Food Network's *Too Hot Tamales*. She competed on season 3 of Bravo's *Top Chef Masters*, making it to the finale and winning forty thousand dollars for her charity, Share Our Strength.

PIE DOUGH

1¾ cups all-purpose flour, plus more for rolling out the dough

½ cup cornstarch

¼ cup vegetable shortening or lard

8 tablespoons (1 stick) unsalted butter

¾ teaspoon kosher salt

1 tablespoon sugar

½ cup ice water

FILLING

2½ pounds rhubarb stalks

1¼ cups sugar, or more to taste if the rhubarb is particularly sour

Whipped cream, for serving, optional

3 tablespoons Minute tapioca

1 In a large bowl, combine the flour, cornstarch, shortening, butter, salt, and sugar. Mix lightly with your fingertips until the dough forms pea-size pieces. You should be able to see chunks of fat. Stir in the water and lightly knead until the dough forms a ball. It is important to handle this dough as little as possible.

2 Form the dough into two 1-inch-thick disks, with one using two-thirds of the dough and the other disk using the remaining one-third of the dough. Transfer the dough disks to a plastic bag. Seal the bag, pressing out any air, and refrigerate for at least 1 hour and up to 3 days, or freeze for up to 1 week. To thaw before use, remove the piecrust from the freezer. Let it sit on the counter for 30 minutes before baking.

3 To assemble the pie, soften the larger dough disk by pressing it in your hands until malleable. On a generously floured board, roll from the center out, lifting the dough, turning it slightly, and occasionally flipping it to prevent sticking. Roll out the dough to a $1/8$-inch thickness. Line a 10-inch pie plate with the dough. Trim dough, leaving about $1/4$-inch overhang for shrinkage. Pinch up excess dough to form a rim. Flute the edges by pressing the thumb of one hand between the thumb and first finger of the other to form a V pattern. Refrigerate the dough in the pie plate for 1 hour.

4 Add the scraps to the smaller disk of dough and roll it out to form an 11-inch circle $1/8$ inch thick. Place it on a plate and refrigerate for 1 hour.

5 Wash the rhubarb, trim it, and cut it crosswise into $1/2$-inch slices. Combine it with the sugar in a large bowl and let it sit at room temperature for 15 minutes. Sprinkle on the tapioca, toss well, and let sit for 15 minutes more.

6 Adjust the oven racks so that one is in the middle for the pie and a second rack is below it. Place a sheet pan on the lower rack to catch drips. Preheat the oven to 400°F. Line the pie plate with a sheet of parchment paper or aluminum foil larger than the plate and add a layer of pie weights or uncooked rice or beans. Bake for 25 minutes, until lightly browned. Remove the weights and paper or foil and set aside.

7 Reduce the heat to 350°F.

8 Use a small knife to cut decorative air vents into the cold top pastry.

9 Pour the rhubarb filling into the warm pie shell. Lay the top crust over it and use a fork to crimp the edges. Bake until the crust is golden brown and the juices bubble, about 75 minutes.

10 Cool on a rack for 30 minutes before serving. Serve plain or, if desired, with whipped cream.

11 Store leftover pie, covered, on the countertop for up to 4 days.

SOUR CREAM CUTOUT COOKIES

Makes about 3 dozen cookies, depending on the cutter size

This recipe came out of Germany on my mother's side, and is attributed to one of my great-grandmothers, who was long gone by the time I came around. Not only does it yield really thick, soft cookies, but the addition of nutmeg and sour cream seems to make these feel more like a riff on a cake than a traditional sugar cookie.

In my family, this recipe is pulled out for every holiday the makers of cookie cutters and Hallmark cards can come up with. I have distinct memories of decorating oddly shaped Santas and perfecting the colored sugar line to make plaid shamrocks. And today, as my daughter reminds me, if I can't find a shape we want, I can just make one out of tin.

These are best if not overbaked. Watch the first few batches closely to figure out the magic amount of time they need in your oven.

4^1/$_2$ cups all-purpose flour, plus more for rolling out the dough

2 teaspoons baking powder

1 teaspoon baking soda

1 teaspoon ground nutmeg

^{1}/$_4$ teaspoon kosher salt

1 cup shortening

2 cups sugar

1 cup full-fat sour cream

2 large eggs, at room temperature

Muriel's Frosting (recipe follows)

1 In a large bowl, combine the flour, baking powder, baking soda, nutmeg, and salt.

2 In another large bowl, cream the shortening and sugar. Add the sour cream and eggs and mix until smooth. Add the dry mixture to the wet mixture and mix until smooth.

3 Cover the dough and refrigerate for at least 1 hour or up to 12 hours. (Seriously, the dough is way too soft to work into shapes without this step!)

4 Preheat the oven to 350°F.

5 On a floured surface, roll out the dough to ^{1}/$_4$ inch thick. Use cookie cutters (or the rim of a glass) to cut out shapes of your choice. Place them on a baking sheet, leaving 2 inches between the cookies.

6 Bake for 9 to 12 minutes, watching closely to be sure you don't overbake. Look for a pale golden brown along the bottom. Let cool completely on wire racks.

7 To lock in freshness, frost the bottoms within 1 day of baking. The "top" of the cookie becomes the "bottom." My parents used to debate whether to frost the top or the bottom of the cookie for freshness. My mom won. Because she was right!

8 Store the cookies in an airtight container for up to 10 days.

❯❯❯❯❯

MURIEL'S FROSTING

Makes 2 cups frosting

This frosting is a simple classic begged off my mother-in-law and her sister that came from their mother, Muriel Meyer. John was really close to his maternal grandparents, so I'm thrilled to include this recipe and combine it with one from my family.

3 tablespoons unsalted butter, softened

1½ teaspoons pure vanilla extract

2 cups powdered sugar

3 tablespoons milk, plus more as needed

In a large bowl, cream the butter and vanilla. Add the powdered sugar and 1 tablespoon of the milk. Mix, adding the remaining 2 tablespoons (or more) of milk as you go until the frosting is thick but pours in an opaque, slow ribbon when spooned up.

Note: If you need to set aside the frosting for an hour (never longer), keep it at room temperature. If it gets a little stiff, add 1 teaspoon of milk at a time to reconstitute it to a spreadable consistency.

CHERRY-NUT CRUMBLE BARS

Makes 24 bars

Crumbles, like all good desserts, seem to turn out a good chunk better when they're cooked in cast iron. Enameled or seasoned cast iron has become my go-to tool for making large batches of goodies.

Cherry-nut crumble is an ode to a recipe from Ellen, the mother of one of my best friends, Katie, and Katie's sister, Jackie. (Jackie has become my sister-in-law, thereby making my best friend and me sort of related because we share nieces! It's like a second grader's dream come true!) We ate this dessert as children growing up but only at Katie and Jackie's house, because my father is allergic to the nuts in it. One bite takes me straight back to elementary school.

This version of the recipe is the only one I've found to have these particular ingredients. It's worth it. (And Ellen said I could share it!)

½ pound (2 sticks) unsalted butter, at room temperature

1 cup granulated sugar

1 teaspoon almond extract

2 large eggs

2 cups all-purpose flour

1 cup canned cherry pie filling

½ cup finely chopped walnuts

¾ cup powdered sugar

1 Preheat the oven to 350°F.

2 In a large bowl, cream the butter and granulated sugar, then mix in the almond extract and eggs. Stir in the flour and mix until smooth.

3 Pour half the batter into a 9 × 13-inch clay baking pan or 12-inch cast-iron skillet and spread it out evenly along the bottom of the pan. Spread the cherry pie filling over the top to cover the bottom layer. Top the filling with the remaining batter, smooth to cover the cherries, and sprinkle the walnuts evenly on top.

4 Bake for 40 minutes, until the cherries bubble and the nuts look toasted.

5 Let cool almost completely, then sprinkle on the powdered sugar. Cut into 24 squares.

6 Store the cherry-nut bars in an airtight container at room temperature for up to 6 days.

AMISH APPLE PIE

Makes one 10-inch pie

I grew up near a lot of Amish and Mennonite farmers (yes, they live in Wisconsin, too). One of my favorite memories is going to one of their local stores to purchase dry-good foodstuffs. The place always smells the same: new warm cheese, green vegetables from their garden, a comforting mix of familiar spices like thyme and rosemary and garlic salt and something fresh and earthy that can be found only on a farm. I admit I still make a special trip there every time I drive the three hours back to Stratford, just to keep the tradition going, even though I can buy anything they have in the stores closer to the cities. There's something so deeply satisfying about shopping at Maranatha Market.

Apple pie is simple, too, so every fall, when the leaves are starting to turn, I make this pie with homemade crust and bake it in a deep dish. It's always a winner!

FILLING

1 cup granulated sugar

3 tablespoons all-purpose flour

1 teaspoon ground cinnamon

1 cup evaporated milk

1 unbaked piecrust (see page 230)

1 teaspoon pure vanilla extract

1 large egg

5 to 7 large McIntosh apples
(5 to 6 pounds, or 1/2 peck)

STREUSEL TOPPING

1/3 cup granulated sugar

1/4 cup packed light brown sugar

1/2 cup plus 2 tablespoons
all-purpose flour

2 teaspoons ground cinnamon

2 teaspoons ground nutmeg

Dash of kosher salt

4 tablespoons (1/2 stick) butter,
cut into 1/2-inch cubes

1 Preheat the oven to 400°F.

2 Make the filling: In a large bowl, combine the granulated sugar, flour, and cinnamon. Add the evaporated milk, vanilla, and egg and stir until combined.

3 Peel the apples, core them, and cut them into 1/4-inch slices. (If needed, keep them in a bowl of salt water or lemon water until you're ready to use them.)

4 Lay the cut apples in the piecrust and pour the wet filling mixture over the apples.

5 Bake for 20 minutes at 400°F. The crust will be pale golden.

6 While the filling is baking, make the streusel topping. Mix the sugars, flour, cinnamon, nutmeg, and salt in a medium bowl.

7 Add the butter to the streusel topping and cut in using a pastry blender or two butter knives.

8 Sprinkle the streusel topping over the pie. Reduce the heat to 350°F and bake for 55 to 60 minutes, until the top puffs up and the apples are soft.

9 Let the pie cool to room temperature before serving.

10 Store leftover pie, covered, at room temperature or in the refrigerator for up to 7 days.

PINEAPPLE UPSIDE-DOWN CAKE

By Erin Connell ● Makes 12 servings

A proud native Oregonian, Erin Connell has been curious about food from an early age. She learned to garden and preserve foods, to catch crabs and clams, and to pick the mushrooms and berries of the Pacific Northwest.

Erin offers us a recipe cooked in her cast iron, stemming from an heirloom memory. Her family often camped on Crescent Lake in Oregon. One year, her aunts and cousins each made something over the fire. Erin's aunt Vicki's pineapple upside-down cake really stood out. The fruit had caramelized nicely, and the cake was so moist! Whenever she makes this cake, she remembers a day of reuniting with family, playing hard, and sitting under the stars.

1 ripe pineapple	1/2 teaspoon kosher salt
1/2 cup coconut oil	6 tablespoons (3/4 stick) unsalted butter
3/4 cup packed light brown sugar	1 cup granulated sugar
1/2 cup light rum	3 large eggs
1 1/2 cups all-purpose flour	1 teaspoon pure vanilla extract
1/4 cup vanilla pudding mix	1/2 cup pineapple juice
2 teaspoons baking powder	1/2 cup macadamia nuts, chopped

1 Set an oven rack in the middle of the oven and preheat the oven to 350°F.

2 Trim the top and bottom off the pineapple and cut off the skin. Halve the pineapple vertically and cut off the woody core. Lay the pineapple halves on a cutting board and cut them crosswise into 1/2-inch slices. You will use approximately 12 slices. (Leftover pineapple slices can be stored in an airtight container in the refrigerator for up to 5 days.)

3 Melt the coconut oil in a 10-inch cast-iron pan over medium heat. (Note: You may want to preheat the cast iron on the stove for 5 minutes before adding the oil in order to maximize the properties of cast iron; just be ready to stand back a bit when the oil hits the pan.) Add the brown sugar and 1/4 cup of the rum and cook, stirring, until the sugar is dissolved, about 3 minutes. Arrange the pineapple slices in the pan in a wheel formation. Set aside in the pan.

4 In a medium bowl, whisk together the flour, pudding mix, baking powder, and salt.

5 In the bowl of a stand mixer with the paddle attachment, cream the butter and granulated sugar on medium speed until light in color and fluffy, about 4 minutes, scraping down the sides of the bowl occasionally while mixing. Add the eggs one at a time, incorporating each fully before adding the next. Add the vanilla and the remaining $1/4$ cup of rum. Add half the dry mixture and mix until incorporated, then add the pineapple juice and the rest of the dry mix.

6 Fold in the nuts by hand. Pour the batter evenly over the pineapple slices sitting in the waiting skillet.

7 Bake until a wooden skewer just comes out clean, 25 to 30 minutes. Set the pan aside to cool a little.

8 When you can hold the skillet without burning yourself, invert a 12-inch heat-safe plate over the skillet and hold it in place with your fingers. Carefully flip the skillet upside down onto the serving platter in one swift movement, lowering the whole setup to a table. Carefully lift the skillet off the cake.

9 Slice and serve at room temperature.

10 Store leftover cake in an airtight container in the refrigerator for up to 2 days.

HOUSE-MADE ALMOND-MILK HOT CHOCOLATE

By Natasha Feldman ● Makes 4 servings

This is one of those recipes that's worth all the work. Natasha has created a wonderful version of a drink that is a staple in Wisconsin winters, as well as on chill fall evenings. Creating homemade almond milk is an extra bonus—it means lots of people can enjoy it for future recipes, too. Be sure to have some marshmallows on hand for garnish!

ALMOND MILK

1/3 cup raw almonds

2 cups filtered water

1/2 teaspoon pure vanilla extract, plus more if needed

Big pinch of kosher salt, plus more if needed

HOT CHOCOLATE

3/4 cup full-fat coconut milk

2 1/4 cups unsweetened almond milk

1 tablespoon cocoa powder

1/2 cup chocolate chips

1/4 cup cacao nibs (optional)

2 tablespoons honey

Pinch of kosher salt

1/2 teaspoon pure vanilla extract

ALMOND MILK

1 You can soak the almonds one of two ways. Ideally you soak them overnight in the refrigerator in water to cover. In a pinch, heat a pan of water to a simmer, turn off the heat, and soak the almonds for 30 minutes.

2 After soaking, drain and rinse the almonds. Place them in a blender and add the filtered water, vanilla, and salt. Blend on high until the mixture looks like milk.

3 Place two layers of cheesecloth over a large bowl (or use a nut milk straining bag if you have one).

4 Slowly pour the almond mixture through the cheesecloth. Wring out the almonds until there is no more liquid released. (You can store the leftover almond meal in an airtight container in the refrigerator for up to 5 months. You can also use the leftover almond meal in another recipe, such as a smoothie or flourless chocolate chip almond cookies.)

5 Taste the milk and add vanilla and/or salt if needed.

6 Store the almond milk in the refrigerator in a capped vessel (a mason jar works fine) for up to 3 days.

HOT CHOCOLATE

1 In a small saucepan, combine the coconut milk, 1/4 cup of the almond milk, and the cocoa powder. Bring to a boil over medium heat.

2 Place the chocolate chips, cacao nibs, honey, salt, and vanilla in a blender.

3 Pour the hot liquid into the blender and let it sit until the chocolate chips are melted.

4 Mix on a low speed until well incorporated. Let sit in the blender.

5 In a small pot, heat the remaining 2 cups of almond milk over medium-low heat.

6 Pour the hot almond milk into the blender with the hot chocolate base.

7 Blend or whip until frothy. Enjoy hot.

8 Store leftover hot chocolate in an airtight container in the refrigerator for up to 1 week.

ALSO BY SARA DAHMEN

Widow 1881

Tinsmith 1865

To learn more about Sara's cookware line, visit House Copper & Cookware www.housecopper.com.

For more information, visit www.saradahmen.com.

Check out the super-cool vintage blocks of tea in the pie plate! Did you know that's how tea used to be sold? Big or small compressed blocks of loose leaves! *This* is what the colonists put in the harbor of Boston.

PRODUCT RESOURCES

There are many companies across the world and right here in the United States that will offer information on the makeup of their cookware and any other questions you might have. While the following list is by no means comprehensive, I hope you'll find it to be a solid leaping-off point for tracking down local cookware artisans. You may find a gem, and its creator, at a local craft fair or market, or you may do as I did and start your research on the internet—you'd be surprised by what you can find in your own backyard. Enjoy the fun of stocking your kitchen with real, heirloom wares that'll last you a few lifetimes and will never need to be deposited in a landfill. Happy hunting!

COPPER
Sara's cookware line, House Copper & Cookware: www.housecopper.com
Brooklyn Copper Cookware: www.brooklyncoppercookware.com
Blanc Creatives: www.blanccreatives.com
Ben & Lael: www.benandlael.com
Mauviel: www.mauvielusa.com
Ruffoni: www.ruffoni.net

IRON
Sara's cookware line, House Copper & Cookware: www.housecopper.com
American Skillet Company: www.americanskilletcompany.com
Lodge Cast Iron: www.lodgemfg.com
Blu Skillet Ironware: www.bluskilletironware.com
Butter Pat Industries: www.butterpatindustries.com
Nest Homeware: www.nesthomeware.com
Le Creuset: www.lecreuset.com
Field Company: www.fieldcompany.com
FINEX Cast Iron Cookware Co.: www.finexusa.com

CLAY
Sara's cookware line, House Copper & Cookware: www.housecopper.com
Rowe Pottery Works: www.rowepottery.com
Ohio Stoneware: www.ohiostoneware.com
Cedar Creek Pottery: www.cedarcreekpottery.com
TR Pottery: www.trpottery.com
Gravesco Pottery: www.gravescopottery.com
Shanel Pottery: West Bend, WI
Brown County Pottery: 58 West Franklin Street, Nashville, IN 47448

FOR FURTHER READING

Here are some resources for those who are as obsessed as I am about cookware, cooking, metalsmithing, and more!

Book of Old-Time Trades and Tools. Mineola, NY: Dover, 2005. Originally published as *The Boy's Book of Trades and the Tools Used in Them*, 1866.

Brandt, Daniel A. *Metallurgy Fundamentals*. South Holland, IL: Goodheart-Willcox, 1992.

Broemel, L., and J. S. Daugherty. *Sheet Metal Workers' Manual*. Chicago: Frederick J. Drake, 1942.

Cabre, Monique. *French Kitchenware*. Paris: L'Aventurine, 2000.

"Copper: An Ancient Metal." Dartmouth Toxic Metals Superfund Research Program. https://sites.dartmouth.edu/toxmetal/more-metals/copper-an-ancient-metal/.

Fuller, John, Sr. *The Art of Coppersmithing: A Practical Treatise on Working Sheet Copper into All Forms*. Lakeville, MN: Astragal Press, 1993. Originally published 1894.

Grass, Gregor, Christopher Rensing, and Marc Solioz. "Metallic Copper as an Antimicrobial Surface." *American Society for Microbiology* 77, no. 5 (2010): 1541–47.

Jaffe, Bernard. *Crucibles: The Story of Chemistry from Ancient Chemistry to Nuclear Fission*. New York: Simon & Schuster, 1948.

Kauffman, Henry J. *American Copper & Brass*. Morgantown, PA: Masthof Press, 1995. Originally published 1968.

Kelley, D. W. *Charcoal and Charcoal Burning*. Buckinghamshire, UK: Shire, 1986.

Lelegren, Shay. *The Complete Tinsmith & Tinman's or Tinner's Trade*. Tinsmith Museum of America, 2016.

McCreight, Tim. *The Complete Metalsmith: An Illustrated Handbook*. Worcester, MA: Davis, 1991.

———. *Practical Casting*. Cape Elizabeth, ME: Brynmorgen Press, 1986.

McRaven, Charles. *The Blacksmith's Craft: A Primer of Tools & Methods*. Storey, 2005. First printing in 1981 as *Country Blacksmithing*.

Moran, Bruce T. *Distilling Knowledge: Alchemy, Chemistry, and the Scientific Revolution*. Cambridge, MA: Harvard University Press, 2005.

Renard, Jean-Claude. *Les cuivres de cuisine*. Paris: Les Éditions de l'Amateur, 1997.

Smith, B. Webster. *Sixty Centuries of Copper*. London: Hutchinson, 1965.

Smith, David G., and Wafford, Chuck. *The Book of Griswold & Wagner*. 2nd ed. Atglen, PA: Schiffer, 2000.

Tyler, John. *Early American Cast Iron Holloware: Pots, Kettles, Teakettles, and Skillets, 1645–1900*. Atglen, PA: Schiffer, 2013.

ACKNOWLEDGMENTS

This book began, like so many other ideas, as a fragment of a conversation. Building a coppersmithing trade over the years, I've been outlandishly fortunate to have mentors for every phase of the process, plus the incredible support of family and friends.

I can't get much further without mentioning Bob Bartelme of Backwoods Tin & Copper, who took me under his wing and made me his official apprentice at his tin shop in Wisconsin. For years, I've been going to the shop multiple times each week (barring kid issues or illness!). The time flies something fierce when we're working on patterns. I still mess up, and Bob can fix it about 99.9 percent of the time. And I am thankful for his wife, Marilyn, who helps out with the kiddos when Bob and I are distracted by machines. Also, she reads all my books. Their entire family has adopted us, and we are included in everything. It's just like the old days, and I (and my family) are forever grateful!

To Uncle Doug, who literally forged the way for someone else in the family to take up metalsmithing. I will use his tools, books, and as much knowledge as I can remember in his memory.

Mac Kohler of Brooklyn Copper Cookware has been a mentor from the start and was extremely supportive of this book idea. Without his guidance, none of the House Copper wares would have existed beyond my napkin sketches.

My family—both extended and blood—has been integral in this process. My parents (Diane and Allie) and my in-laws (Jerilyn and Gary) have watched the kiddos, folded laundry, traveled, and even singed their clothes and eyebrows throughout this endeavor (on the cookware, not the book). My husband, John, and I could not have managed half of what's on these pages without their love and acceptance of our crazy life.

Everyone who is interviewed in *Copper, Iron, and Clay* or who supplied recipes holds a place in my heart: Mary Sue, Lisa, John and Renee, Erin, Natasha, and Beth—the food is fantastic! I know because I cooked it all! And again, Mary Sue, plus Giulia, Henry, Valérie, Mac, Bob, Dan, Norb, Erik, Brad, Rebekah, Bev, and Alisa—thank you for putting down your personal thoughts, words of wisdom, and stories in these pages. Also, thank you to all the myriad people in the wings who made these interviews happen at all! I'm forever thankful and grateful. All the family-owned companies that helped me build the House Copper & Cookware line are indispensable for their advice and their support. And I'd be remiss if I didn't give a shoutout to all the guys at the tinsmith convergence (including Bob), who always give me their two cents when I ask a dozen questions. They are salt of the earth, and they're truly brilliant.

Christian, Elle May, and Hanna of 1924 US and Nicole Styles—you guys know how impossible the photography would be without your styling and vision and final touches. Craig Anderson, my first, ground-floor editor, who understands my work, my voice, and what makes me tick, pushed to make this book less dry and more entertaining—thank you for making it more approachable and not something that puts you to sleep!

A thanks to the talented Leah Carlson-Stanisic for the lovely interior layout of this book (I can't believe it's really here!) and Jeanne Reina for the cover design (you nailed it!).

To Bonnie Nadell, my agent, who understood exactly what I wanted to say and was up for doing the work to make it happen, fighting for the big vision the whole way (and to Rachel Feldman, who told me to talk to Bonnie, and to Natasha, who introduced me to Rachel!), and to Cassie Jones, my sister from another Wisconsin mother at William Morrow, who completely supported this book and beyond from day one—I love you guys. Let's do it all!

I'm grateful to my friends, whom I drag to my house for "appetizers that may or may not be like a photoshoot dinner party, I mean, can you wear neutral colors, please?" and allow their children to stay up late while we eat, drink, and take gorgeous photos. Melissa and Dave, Julia and Justin, Nicole and Jason, and Andi and Brian, thanks for making shooting this book so much fun and for pretending we don't have seventeen children among us all. The frog didn't die in the lemon squeezer, no one forgot a child when leaving the house, and who cares if the cake was store bought because it photographed perfectly. And Julia, thanks extra for always brainstorming over coffee or mimosas after yoga on the patio.

Though I am sure I'm forgetting about a hundred people, I need to thank my children, Will, Hannah, and Jack, for letting me, without a mutter of reproof, jet-set around the country to get this book made, people met, and photos taken. And finally, and most important, thank you to John, who is my other half and other skin. I wouldn't be who I am today, doing what I'm doing, if I hadn't been fortunate enough to make a match with you.

Let's live to be 102, okay?

INDEX

Note: Page references in *italics* indicate recipe photographs.

COPPER, IRON, AND CLAY. Copyright © 2020 by Sara Dahmen. All rights reserved. Printed in Canada. No part of this book may be used or reproduced in any manner whatsoever without written permission except in the case of brief quotations embodied in critical articles and reviews. For information, address HarperCollins Publishers, 195 Broadway, New York, NY 10007.

HarperCollins books may be purchased for educational, business, or sales promotional use. For information, please email the Special Markets Department at SPsales@harpercollins.com.

FIRST EDITION

Designed by Leah Carlson-Stanisic

Interior photography by Christian Watson and Elle May Watson, 1924 US, except the following: pages 2, 37, 39, 42, 81, 121, 136, 159, 181, 197, 204, 206, 234, and 239 courtesy of the author; pages 6, 10, 26, 29, 58, 60, and 87 by Nicole Styles, Nicole Style Photography; page 15 by Lane Goldstone; page 68 by Mauviel; page 78 courtesy of Giulia Ruffoni; page 91 by Peter Undiks; page 130 by Bob Hodson; page 150 by Eric & Sarah Lang, Lovely Ember Photography; page 156 by Lodge Manufacturing Marketing Department; pages 216 and 219 by Julia Behm, Design Between; page 231 by Mary Sue Milliken

---

Library of Congress Cataloging-in-Publication Data

Names: Dahmen, Sara, author.

Title: Copper, iron, and clay : a Smith's journey / Sara Dahmen.

Description: First edition. | New York, NY : William Morrow, an imprint of HarperCollins Publishers, 2020. | Includes bibliographical references and index. | Summary: "A gorgeously photographed love letter to copper pots, cast-iron skillets, and classic stoneware and the hard-won artistry that goes into them, by perhaps the only woman coppersmith in the country"-- Provided by publisher.

Identifiers: LCCN 2019054665 (print) | LCCN 2019054666 (ebook) | ISBN 9780062943736 | ISBN 9780062943743 (digital edition)

Subjects: LCSH: Cookware. | Metal-work. | Copper. | Cast-iron. | Stoneware. | Cooking.

Classification: LCC TX657.C74 D34 2020 (print) | LCC TX657.C74 (ebook) | DDC 643/.3--dc23

LC record available at https://lccn.loc.gov/2019054665

LC ebook record available at https://lccn.loc.gov/2019054666

ISBN 978-0-06-294373-6

20 21 22 23 24 ITIB 10 9 8 7 6 5 4 3 2 1